ILLINOIS WINES
& WINERIES

ILLINOIS
WINES & WINERIES
The Essential Guide

CLARA ORBAN

SOUTHERN ILLINOIS UNIVERSITY PRESS • Carbondale

17 16 15 14   4 3 2 1

Book and cover design by Linda Jorgensen Buhman

Library of Congress Cataloging-in-Publication Data
Orban, Clara Elizabeth, [date]
Illinois wines and wineries : the essential guide / Clara Orban.
   pages cm
Includes index.
ISBN 978-0-8093-3344-8 (paperback)
ISBN 0-8093-3344-9 (paperback)
ISBN 978-0-8093-3345-5 (ebook)
1. Wine and wine making—Illinois. I. Title.
TP557.5.I3O73 2014
338.4'7663209773—dc23   2013046870

The paper used in this publication meets the minimum requirements
of American National Standard for Information Sciences—Permanence
of Paper for Printed Library Materials, ANSI Z39.48-1992. ∞

Cover image, photo from iStock; *Frontispiece*, The state of Illinois, with
county seats; *Title page*, photo from iStock.com; *Page 42*, Pinot Noir grapes
at Valentino Vineyards, photographed by Rudolph Valentino, courtesy of
Valentino Vineyards and Winery; *Page 43*, Northern wine region; *Page 82*,
Alto's Chambourcin grapes, photo courtesy of Alto Vineyards; *Page 83*,
Central wine region; *Page 108*, Vignoles grapes, photo courtesy of Megan
Presnall/IGGVA; *Page 109*, South central wine region; *Page 144*, Cabernet
grapes at Valentino Vineyards, photographed by Rudolph Valentino, courtesy
of Valentino Vineyards and Winery; *Page 145*, Southern wine region. All
maps courtesy of Jill Thomas.

Contents

Acknowledgments

This book was born from a rejection letter, as it turned out one of the happier coincidences of my life thus far. My previous book, *Wine Lessons: Ten Questions to Guide Your Appreciation of Wine*, had to find a home (it has since done so, with Kendall Hunt Publishing). Southern Illinois University Press seemed like the ideal connection since the last chapter includes a "postcard from the harvest" at Kite Hill Vineyards in southern Illinois. Karl Kageff, editor in chief at Southern Illinois University Press, felt that book would be outside the scope of the SIU Press's marketing strategies.

In his rejection letter, he did, however, ask whether I would consider a guidebook to Illinois wine. Undoubtedly this was a great interest of mine already, so I decided to send in a proposal. My first debt of gratitude, therefore, goes to Karl for having wondered out loud if this type of book might be in my range. Amy Etcheson and Barb Martin of Southern Illinois University Press have been wonderful promoting the book even before it was ready for the outside world to read, and with their editing expertise, Wayne K. Larsen and Kathy Kageff did a superb job helping me eliminate as many errors as possible from this text. I also thank Dan Palumbo for working so quickly to give me a hand with the copyedited manuscript.

I have since learned that two eminent Illinois food and wine experts were the peer reviewers for this work. I would like to thank Bruce Kraig for believing in this proposal and telling Southern Illinois University Press that the proposal had merit. Since then, he has also put me in touch with the Greater Midwest Foodways Alliance, a group of writers and food experts who, like me, want to share the riches of this great part of the country with readers and audiences.

Paul Renzaglia, from one of the most important families of Illinois wine, was also a reader who approved of my proposal for this book. He has been a great source of information on Illinois wine, and I thank him for his interest in the book as well as in helping me compile it. His enthusiasm for Illinois wine, and for helping promote the great producers here, is inspiring.

The Illinois Grape Growers and Vintners Association (IGGVA) has been extremely helpful in gathering information, and their website includes valuable information on Illinois wines. I have a great debt to them for much of the information in this book. Megan Presnall and Bill McCartney responded to e-mails and phone calls as I made sure I featured the wineries in appropriate categories. They are professionals who love promoting Illinois wine, and I'm happy if this book can help them in their work. The list of wineries profiled in this book comes from the IGGVA website. The staff told me that they know of most of the wineries of the state, but wineries are not obligated to report to them, as they are to the liquor board. In his online publication *Midwest Wine Press* (April 24, 2013), Mark Ganchiff noted that there were 126 Illinois wineries, but that the IGGVA lists ninety-nine. The IGGVA notes that wineries that have closed but still hold their federal permit or wineries that are starting but not open yet account for most of the differences. Of courses, it is in a winery's best interest to take advantage of the marketing potential provided by the IGGVA. For that reason, I concluded that basing this book on the wineries they have on file for the state of Illinois would give the most complete guide. The wineries in this book represent the May 2013 IGGVA list. For that reason, some newer wineries may have been left out. Also, some wineries may have closed their doors. Do check in advance to see if wineries are open before making a trip.

Megan Presnall at the IGGVA. *Author's collection.*

The state lobbyist David Stricklin and his assistant Danielle D'Alessandro helped me find wines to bring to conferences so that I could show tangible proof to interested audiences of the quality of Illinois wines.

Mark Ganchiff, a real expert and enthusiast of midwestern wine making, has been invaluable in helping me get to know Illinois wine. His online publication *Midwest Wine Press*, mentioned above, is a rich resource of information for anyone interested in learning about wines from all parts of the midwestern region. Mark was also invaluable in providing excellent feedback on the manuscript as a reviewer for SIU Press and in his help with photos to illustrate it.

The vintners themselves of Illinois have been very helpful in creating this book. Many of them answered questionnaires and provided illustrations included here. I hope this book will help them publicize their talents.

My colleagues James Montgomery and John Tandarich were very helpful in gathering more information about Illinois soil.

Mary and Bill Slider, fast friends and fellow travelers, have been instrumental in introducing two "northerners" to the lovely southern part of the state that for them as well is an adopted home. Without them, the wines of Illinois would still be somewhat of a mystery to me.

Photo credits have been interspersed throughout the book.

In the course of writing books through the years, on many various topics, family and friends have been most important in keeping me sane(r). I thank Dan Mulvihill, devotee of the Illinois State Fair, for helping disseminate questionnaires at that event despite his having a full agenda of other activities. My husband, Elliot Weisenberg, has accompanied me on many trips throughout the state as we explored Illinois wines together. He and I have come to know much more of this wonderful state and are certainly the richer for it. To him, as always, I dedicate this book.

ILLINOIS WINES & WINERIES

Alto Vineyards' first harvest. *Courtesy of Alto Vineyards.*

1.
Illinois Wine History

"*T*he Prairie State."
"Land of Lincoln."
"Oenotria"?
We know Illinois deserves its reputation as the Prairie State thanks to the beautiful expanse of prairie that covered it before European settlers came. Thankfully this habitat is being lovingly revived in small parcels by enthusiastic environmentalists.

We know Illinois deserves its reputation as the Land of Lincoln because, although the sixteenth president of the United States was born in Kentucky, he began his legal career in Illinois and represented Illinois in Washington, D.C., before his election as president.

But Oenotria, in Ancient Greek, "the land of staked (or piled) vines"? That's not a term we usually associate with Illinois. It was the name ancient Greeks gave to Italy, precisely the island of Sicily, when they founded cities to create a golden age of science and art on the Italian peninsula. Italy, a country where 80 percent of the geography can support grape growing, has a tradition of wine making going back several thousand years. Italy claims the title "Land of Staked Vines."

Illinois is a relative newcomer to the tradition of wine making. But the enthusiasm of Illinois vintners, with their passion for producing a quality product that will be admired and shared, is limitless. In this book, then, we will take a journey through what, at least temporarily, we will rename "Illinois, Land of the Grape."

When we think of wines in the United States, we think first of California. It has almost always been that way. Father Juniper Serra, Franciscan monk, planted vines near the missions he established throughout the state in the late 1700s. By the mid-1800s, California had an extensive wine-making culture, which only increased thanks to the demand for alcohol during the Gold Rush of 1848. California still today is the largest producer of wine in the United States. But Illinois wine has a long tradition, dating back to the first settlers. In fact Illinois was among the largest producers of wine, that is, until Prohibition.

The Eighteenth Amendment, ratified in 1919, had a chilling effect on production of alcohol in this country. The Volstead Act established enforcement of the amendment but allowed for medicinal, sacramental, and home production in limited quantities. All wine-producing areas suffered and took decades to come back after Prohibition's repeal on December 5, 1933.

If we start at the beginning of Illinois history, we know that agriculture was a part of the lives of the earliest native tribes in this area. While Plains Indians had long traditions of hunting and gathering; the Illinois area was also home to native tribes that built elaborate cities. When humans congregate in large groups, inevitably some forms of agriculture must be cultivated to sustain the population because hunting and gathering is rarely enough. Cahokia, near the Mississippi River adjacent to what is today St. Louis, was a pre-Columbian culture that built a vast cityscape still visible in the form of mounds. This Cahokia Native American group, however, died out for mysterious reasons.

Today's Illinois was subsequently home to the Illiniwek Confederation. They were displaced by the expansion of the Iroquois Nation and thereafter left their place to the Pottawatomie, Miami, Sauk, and other tribes. All these groups mixed hunting, gathering, and agriculture to survive.

We doubt, however, that wine was among their crops. There were indigenous grapevines in the territory of Illinois, but we do not have evidence of

Fox Valley's vineyard. *Courtesy of Fox Valley Winery, Inc.*

fermentation. In the Ancient Icelandic saga *Vinland*, the Norsemen wrote of finding vines in the Northeast, around today's Newfoundland. We know, therefore, of indigenous grapes in North America (*Vitis labrusca* genus). However, there is little evidence the Plains Native Americans produced or consumed grape wine.

Propitious, perhaps, for the expansion of viticulture in Illinois, the first European explorers to this area were French. Jacques Marquette and Louis Jolliet, who explored the Mississippi in 1673, were thus the first to arrive in present-day Illinois. The French would have a great influence in these earliest years. René-Robert Cavelier, Sieur de La Salle, and Henry de Tonti arrived in 1680 and built Fort Crèvecoeur near Peoria. The late years of the seventeenth century saw many French traders and clergy come to Illinois to establish a flourishing French culture near the Mississippi. By 1779 Jean Baptiste Point du Sable had established a trading post in what today is Chicago. Thus, from the east to the west of the state, there was a French presence.

We know these first settlers found grapes among the plants growing wild. Denis Raudot's *Letters from America* (1710) notes about Illinois:

> The land is almost all flat and smooth. There are no mountains, only a few wooded hills. It is nothing but prairies as far as the eye can see, dotted here and there with small patches of woods, with orchards, and with avenues of trees which it seems as if nature took pleasure in making grow in a straight line equally distant from one another. These woods are full of horse chestnuts, locusts, oaks, ashes, basswoods, beeches, cottonwoods, maples, pecans, mulberries, chestnuts, and plums. All these trees almost covered with a vine that bears a handsome grape and which has large seeds, but has not an agreeable taste.[1]

On February 3, 1809, the Illinois territory was created, and soon after that (1818) Illinois became the twenty-first state. European settlers were already arriving in the area, bringing new crops and ways of farming the very rich soil.

Farming still today in Illinois revolves around crops that need good soil in which to grow: soybeans, corn, wheat, oats, sorghum, and hay. Grapes have come recently to the scene as important ingredients for the flourishing wine industry of Illinois. Cultivation of grapes and wine making is not new to Illinois, but the wine-making industry has taken hold only since the beginning of the twenty-first century. If we trace the history of grapes, it might be useful to reproduce the following timeline which comes from the IGGVA website: http://www.illinoiswine.com/history.html.

---

1. Letter 56: "The Country the Illinois Inhabit, the Trees Found There and the Vegetables Which Are Cultured There—At Quebec 1710," http://www.museum.state.il.us/exhibits/lewis_clark_il/htmls/il_1803/raudot.html. On the Illinois State Museum site go to "Natural Illinois." On the left sidebar you will find "Raudot's Journal." From *The Indians of the Western Great Lakes, 1615–1760*, ed. William Vernon Kinietz, 384–85. Occasional Contributions for the Museum of Anthropology of the University of Michigan. No. 10. Ann Arbor: University of Michigan Press, 1940.

I've added information within the grid to better understand certain key moments:

- 1778—French settlers in La Ville de Maillet (what is now Peoria) bring the wine-making expertise of their homeland to Illinois. The village features a winepress and an underground wine vault.

The oldest recorded grape vineyard—of Concord grapes—was in Nauvoo, Illinois, on the banks of the Mississippi River. That vineyard, by the way, is still producing fruit in Nauvoo State Park. The town became known for its wines in the late 1800s.

- 1857—Emile Baxter and Sons open a winery in Nauvoo, along the banks of the Mississippi River. Baxter's Vineyards remains Illinois' oldest operating winery, run by a fifth generation of Baxters.

The Baxters came back to making wines after Prohibition and were the first bonded winery in the state at that point. They survived Prohibition by shipping grapes north, and making wine only for their own consumption.

- 1900—Illinois is the fourth-largest wine-producing state in the nation.
- 1919—Prohibition prohibits the sale, transport and production of alcohol. The Volstead Act enforces the amendment but allows production of sacramental wine, for example. Some Illinois vineyards continue to grow table grapes; others uproot their vines to make way for corn and soybeans.

We've already alluded to Prohibition and its effect on the wine industry. I cannot emphasize enough how Prohibition changed the landscape, quite literally, of this country. Few other countries have experienced such a dramatic, man-made

Alto Vineyards' first harvest wagon. *Courtesy of Alto Vineyards.*

event launched to influence behavior and that ended up creating unanticipated consequences affecting agriculture and culture. After Prohibition it took decades for wine production to recover. Americans had moved on to consuming hard liquors, beer, and cocktails and were less interested in wine. For several generations wine was relegated to "ethnic" enclaves, communities of immigrants who came from cultures that embraced wines.

- 1979–95—Wineries and vineyards are established throughout the northern, central, and southern regions of Illinois.

Guy Renzaglia became a key figure. A retired professor from Southern Illinois University, Guy established the first vineyard in what is now the Shawnee Hills Wine AVA. Guy's vision led to an explosion of vineyards in that part of the state, which is especially suited to growing grapes. He also began planting hybrid grapes, new varieties such as Chancellor, Chambourcin, Vidal Blanc, and Villard Blanc. For the most part, these are grapes that still today grow best in Illinois.

- 1995—The owners of Alto Vineyards, Owl Creek Vineyards, and Pomona Winery in southern Illinois meet with area tourism officials and form the Shawnee Hills Wine Trail.
- 2001—Illinois boasts twenty-seven wineries.
- 2005—Illinois governor Rod R. Blagojevich designates September as Illinois Wine Month.
- 2006—A region in southern Illinois is recognized as the Shawnee Hills American Viticultural Area (AVA) by the federal government. Illinois' first AVA designation, this area encompasses twenty-one wineries and fifty-five vineyards.
- 2009—The Upper Mississippi River Valley AVA is established, becoming the largest in the United States. This AVA includes regions of Minnesota, Wisconsin, Iowa, and Illinois and represents thirty-two wineries and 445 vineyard acres.

In fall 2012 the Illinois Grape Growers and Vintners Association (IGGVA) released a survey of Illinois' current wine profile. They divided operations into commercial vineyards, vineyard-wineries, and wineries. Total wine production in 2011 was 651,800 gallons. There was a 36 percent increase in commercial wineries between 2006 and 2011, and total

Alto Vineyards' Paul Renzaglia. *Courtesy of Alto Vineyards.*

Lake Hill Winery and Banquet Hall, one of Illinois' newest. *Courtesy of Lake Hill Winery and Banquet Hall.*

wine production increased 16 percent. Almost half, 46 percent, of the wineries surveyed in 2011 were established after 2005. The last years of the first decade of the twenty-first century saw a boom in Illinois wineries and wine production.

In 2013 the Illinois wine industry created a direct economic impact of more than $253 million annually. The wineries that span Illinois have also brought with them a host of charming bed-and-breakfasts and local craft businesses. The IGGVA predicts continued growth in the coming years as more visitors discover the genuine culture of Illinois wine country.

Today there's a generational change in the world of Illinois wine. The second, sometimes third, generation of winemakers has new ideas. On my travels to visit wineries, one young winemaker told me that he and others like him are trying to transform their grandparents' culture of the sweet Concord grape wine to embrace dry, international-style wines. There will surely be new changes in the future for Illinois wine.

I would like to say a few words at the end of this chapter about the IGGVA, a group of dedicated professionals who are promoting Illinois wines. Their office in Springfield puts them in a central location to observe and help nurture new vintners as they continue to catalog the wineries for the state. They have been instrumental in putting together this book.

Illinois, a state known for its agricultural bounty, initially came somewhat late to quality wine making on a commercial scale, but has made up for lost time. The wineries in the state differ in that some grow their own grapes, while others import some or all of their raw materials. Illinois winemakers have capitalized on French American hybrids that adapt more readily to the Illinois climate. They bottle, store, and market their wines in ways familiar to wine lovers everywhere. So while perhaps the title "oenotria" may be somewhat ambitious, grapes now thrive side-by-side with corn on the prairie in the Land of Lincoln.

2.
The Basics of Wine Production

*I*n this brief introduction, we need to explore some of the elements that go into wine production in Illinois. The techniques, materials, and methods will be similar to quality wine making the world over. However, Illinois does present some unique opportunities for exploration with grape varieties because of its soil and climate. We'll touch on some of the information you'll need to begin enjoying Illinois wine and then discuss what makes wines from Illinois special.

STEPS TOWARD FERMENTATION

Alcoholic Fermentation
Grape pulp, skins, juice, and seeds become alcohol in a natural process when water and sugar come in contact with air and yeast. Yeast exists in the wild, so it doesn't need to be added. Saccharomyces, the wild yeast usually found in vineyards, is essential to converting the water and sugar into alcohol. Today, however, in most commercial wineries, wild yeasts are cleaned off so that special yeast can be added into the vat. This allows the winemaker as much control as possible of the entire fermentation process. The final proportion of the process: *2 percent sugar will yield 1 percent alcohol.*

Although some wines mandate a set time for fermentation, or a certain amount of time the skins can be in contact with the juice, the general process always involves extracting the juice from the grapes by crushing or pressing, or both; adding yeast to the mixture; and taking the leftover seeds, leaves, and so on out of the juice before continuing the process. Other steps involved in wine making may include any or all of the following, depending on the wine and the winemaker.

Malolactic Process
Many red wines and a few white wines undergo what is sometimes called "secondary fermentation," really the malolactic process. In this bacterial process,

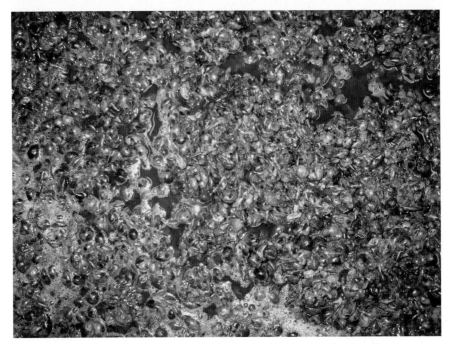

Fermenting juice at Hickory Ridge Vineyard and Winery. *Author's collection.*

Fermentation at Walnut Street Winery. *Courtesy of Walnut Street Winery.*

Scott Albert of Kite Hill Vineyards with just fermented wine. *Author's collection.*

a wine's malic acid (the sharp acid of apples, for example) is converted to lactic acid (the softer acid of milk).

Carbonic Maceration

There is also an alternate fermentation used for wines that need to remain fresh and fruity. The carbonic maceration method puts whole bunches of grapes for a very short time into the fermentation tank with the cap closed. This allows gravity to crush the grapes; the fruit flavor largely remains. Wines produced this way retain their flavor and bright fruit taste.

Cold Soaking

This involves crushing the grapes, letting them soak in a cool place, and then moving them toward bottling after fermentation. This allows extreme color penetration, without extracting too much tannin. It proves ideal for years when the grapes may not be ripe but the wine needs soft tannins. Once the winemaker achieves the desired properties, skins are extracted.

Extended Aging on the Lees

This means allowing the lees—the detritus in the barrel—to remain with the juice for a longer period. According to many winemakers, this provides more nutrients and complexity to the wine.

Micro-oxygenation

With this process, oxygen is pumped into the lees-juice mixture, which also keeps the lees fresher as they give off their nutrients.

Prefermentation and Cold Maceration

This involves cooling the tanks and essentially "soaking" the crushed grapes without oxygen before allowing fermentation to begin. This may increase color without increasing tannins.

Fermenting grapes at Hidden Lake Winery. *Author's collection*.

Sulfites

There is a current controversy surrounding sulfites in wines. In the United States, wine containing more than ten milligrams of sulfites per liter must include a warning label "contains sulfites" because of severe allergic reactions to sulfites (although these are extremely rare). Sulfites are often considered artificial ingredients, but they are actually produced naturally during the fermentation process. Winemakers may add sulfites to wine to prevent spoilage.

AFTER FERMENTATION

Barrel Aging

We now consider that most red wines benefit from barrel aging. The barrel came about when the Roman saw that the Gauls, whom they were conquering, stored their wines in wood containers. Up to that point, the ancient Greeks and Romans had been storing their wines in clay or terra cotta containers, amphorae. Although this was an excellent way to keep the wine cool, especially if the containers were submerged in the ground, this material also leaks. Properly treated wood barrels on the other hand, do not. Plus, for an army such as the Romans' on long marches, wood barrels proved much lighter and easier to carry than heavy amphorae. Still today we use wood barrels for aging most red wines, and some white wine. Illinois winemakers are increasingly embracing aged red wines, and many of those who do usually put that information on the label.

Illinois winemakers tend to age their wines in American, French, or Hungarian oak, depending on the winery and on the desired results. Each of the woods will impart slightly different nuances to the wine. The majority still use American oak, however, if they barrel age their wines. Many producers who want a fresher, more youthful tasting wine swear by American oak. With a slightly more porous texture, American oak may add flavors of vanilla, banana, and coconut to wine.

Barrels are also aged and seasoned in a process that seals the wood to become practically impermeable. Barrels are charred on the inside to a light, medium, or heavy toast. (Lighter wines will need a light toast, for example.)

Fruit Forward

The phenol level in the juice—the tannins—can be controlled by allowing some skin contact with the wine. This will produce what is known as a "fruit forward" wine. For fruit forward results, a winemaker can also try to keep fermentation as cool as possible, at the limit where the yeast will work, but not much more. This means the winemaker can keep the fermentation going and extract maximum fruit flavor. Another way to increase fruitiness is to regulate the barrel size; the more wine you have in the container—that is, the bigger the container—the less the wood will affect the final outcome. Fruit forward wines bring out the fruit characteristics inherent in the grapes. Most Illinois wines are fruit forward.

Terroir

Wines that exhibit *terroir* bring out the mineral characteristics of the soil in which the grapes grow. Each patch of earth, many winemakers believe, imparts characteristics of the diverse layers of different soil through which the grapevines must travel to reach water. European winemakers tend to emphasize terroir. Most Illinois winemakers emphasize fruit forward, as we saw above.

Tannins

Grape skins contain tannins, part of the phenolic class of chemical compounds, which gives wine its structure, or in other words makes the wine almost "chewy." White wines tend to be high in acidity, not unpleasantly so, hopefully, but enough

Barrels stacked and ready to fill at Galena Cellars, Winery, and Vineyard. *Courtesy of Megan Presnall/IGGVA.*

Rows at Creekside Vineyards. *Courtesy of Creekside Vineyards, Winery, and Inn.*

to make the back of your mouth salivate when you drink them. Red wines contain tannins, a substance that creates a texture in your mouth. You may notice that when you drink a red wine, it will leave an effect on the roof of your mouth similar to tea. Tannins are also present in tea leaves, thus the similarity between the two beverages.

Harvesting Chardonnay grapes at Blue Sky Vineyard. *Courtesy of Blue Sky Vineyard.*

Color

Winemakers leave the skins in contact with the juice for red wines to increase tannins, but also to extract color. Grape pulp is almost always white (there are a few grapes with pink flesh known as "teinturier," from a French word for *color*). Wine color almost always comes from the skin. When the liquid is left in contact with the skin, the juice begins to take on not only the tannins, but also the color of the red wine you eventually want to bottle.

VINEYARD MANAGEMENT

We've explored what goes into making wine in the winery. Now we explore important elements in the vineyard. In this book, we will feature several different types of establishments that constitute the rich panorama of Illinois wine. There are several properties that house vineyards but do not have wineries. These are grape growers who sell their grapes to producers but who do not make wine on the premises or under their own labels.

There are also wineries in Illinois, many of them. These may be either winery-vineyards, or simply wineries. Wineries produce wines from grapes using a particular style. Some wineries are also vineyards; they grow grapes to use in producing their own style of wine. Many Illinois wineries use at least part of their own grown grapes in production. I consider winery-vineyards the most complete wine-growing entities. In the case of both wineries and winery-vineyards, most of them are open to the public for tastings, buying, and events.

The section that follows talks about the growing conditions in Illinois as they relate to grapes, and that means this section is of particular interest for understanding the winery-vineyards and the vineyards of Illinois.

Trellising

Like all vines, grapevines will spread as far as you let them. Gardeners who grow tomatoes know you must stake the plants for that reason. Similarly, in almost all parts of the world now, grapevines are fixed to trellises to limit their spread and concentrate flavors in the fruit. It also allows winemakers to limit or extend the sunlight the plants get, depending on need. Some areas of the world still allow

Harvesting trellised grapes at Blue Sky Vineyard. *Courtesy of Blue Sky Vineyard.*

grapes' vines to grow as bushes because of particular climactic concerns (for example, if the plants need more heat from the soil, or if they need less direct sunlight). Still, trellises have been adopted almost everywhere to manage vines. Trellising the plants also regulates the moisture they receive. Winemakers know that if the fruit collects water, the resultant wine will be watery.

Pruning

As with all plants, pruning dead leaves and branches helps concentrate nutrients in the other parts of the plant that may need it more. Grape growers prune the plants in late fall and winter.

Bunch Thinning

We mentioned the need to concentrate the flavors in the individual grapes. This method mandates that less-ripe bunches should be cut off the vine before growing to maturity, so that flavors can concentrate in the remaining bunches. Grape growers use this method to improve the quality of their wines.

Canopy Management

Sunlight is essential to allow grapes to mature. If too many leaves cover the bunches, that becomes more difficult. For that reason, winemakers will often cut off leaves or branches to help bunches get as much sunlight as possible, especially in colder years. Many Illinois grape growers throughout the state use canopy management to help grapes mature.

Excessive Water

In Illinois, access to water for crops is less of an issue than it is in many grape-growing areas such as Australia, for example. However, once again, this may at first be an embarrassment of riches. Grapevines like some stress, and winemakers worldwide are having some success with limiting access to water. Most

Fox Valley Winery and its beautiful rows of grapevines. *Courtesy of Fox Valley Winery, Inc.*

Tractor harvest at Mackinaw Valley Vineyard and Winery. *Courtesy of Larry Lueallen.*

areas famous for wine advertise their "difficult soil," chalk, pebbles, and so on. In the Duoro Valley of Portugal, growers even blast holes in rock to plant their vines. Vines need to go deep to get their water, so even climates with relatively little rainfall can be ideal for grapes. In areas of the world where drought can be a problem, winemakers have resorted at times to "dry viticulture," that is, not irrigating vines at all and allowing only the most resistant to survive.

Illinois has many rivers and lakes that feed the ground, so access to water is usually not an issue for Illinois grape growers (except in drought years such as 2012).

Pests and Disease

The phylloxera louse was perhaps the most destructive pest for the vineyards of the world. It lived peacefully in American vineyards since native American *Vitis labrusca* grapes are not susceptible to it. Phylloxera eats the root of vines; the American species grapes were, however, resistant to it.

To save wine making after the phylloxera attack, Thomas Volnay Munson, an Illinoisan living in Texas, had the idea to graft the vine roots of *Vitis labrusca* to the shaft of a *Vitis vinifera*. He shipped phylloxera resistant rootstocks to help revive the French wine industry. Grafting involves making a diagonal cut into the root, and tying onto it the stalk of another plant, also cut on the diagonal. The two fuse together at the cut and become one plant that can continue to grow. The resultant grapes are *Vitis vinifera*—Chardonnay, Cabernet Sauvignon, Pinot Noir, etc.—and the crop is saved. We can see here the benefits of combining grapes into hybrids, which are the mainstay of the Illinois wine

15

industry. These types of grapes can combine the flavor of *Vitis vinifera* with the robust characteristics of another genus of grapes.

Climate

There are two main climates in which grapes thrive: Mediterranean and Continental. The former is typical of Italy, Greece, the South of France, and California. The latter is typical of New Zealand, Burgundy in France, and Oregon. Illinois is neither. Furthermore, there are many climactic variations in Illinois from north to south. Grapes tend to need warmer climates, so many of the hybrids planted in Illinois are ideal to withstand colder climates.

Illinois represents a climate that can harbor extremes, especially in the northern two thirds of the state. However, *microclimates* can help alleviate these larger climactic hazards. Microclimates are pockets of climate that differ from their surroundings. For example, you may live in a region with much fog and rain, but if you are in an elevated part of this general area, you may get more sunshine, and fewer problems with humidity. The air circulation of the higher elevations may alleviate some of these concerns. Winemakers tend to favor microclimates that can bring benefits to their wines.

Soil

The grapes do need to send roots very far into the soil to get water (the main reason why tropical areas are not ideal for growing grapes and making wine: they are simply too wet). The plants send the roots sometimes eighteen feet below the surface. As the roots bring that water back to the surface, they bring with them nutrients from various depths.

Illinois' soil is extremely rich and varied, and each section of this state has different soil types. Most of the southern, northeastern, and western regions were formed before the glaciers of the last ice age covered parts of the area. The rest was formed by receding glaciers. Glacial deposits tend to be good for agriculture because they have fine soil and are free of rocks. They retain moisture as well. None of these characteristics, however, is essential for grapes.

Most of Illinois has loess soil, which comes from alluvial soils. Illinois and other parts of the upper Midwest were formed when glaciers receded. These glaciers left deposits and ridges throughout what was essentially flat land. In technical language, glaciers leave "drift" behind, that is, deposits more characteristic of lakes. "Mollisols" are common in Illinois, a rich soil created by decomposition of prairie plants. "Alfisols," which develop under forest vegetation, are less fertile and more common in southern Illinois.

Most of Illinois is layers of drift from ancient glaciers, or alluvial soil. This is covered, to differing depths, with loess.

Alluvial: This soil comes from deposits, usually after flooding. One type of soil, often in large quantities, covers existing soils in a region and overlays its characteristics onto the existing bedrock. Alluvial soils tend to be richer in nutrients since they come from a variety of sources.

Loess: This type of soil is a deposit of silt that has spread through wind action. Areas with loess soil usually bordered lakes or continental glaciers. In

Grape juice harvest at Mackinaw Valley Vineyard and Winery. *Courtesy of Larry Lueallen.*

German, "loess" means "crumbly," so that gives you an idea of what the soil looks and feels like as it runs through your fingers.

In many parts of the state, there are remnants of the ice age under our feet. This type of soil is excellent for growing many types of crops. Usually grapes enjoy more difficult soil. Many vineyards worldwide exist in almost desert climates, with rocky soils that the roots need to push through to get water. Illinois has a much richer soil thanks to these millennial deposits from ancient waters.

Topography

Grapes tend to favor hills. Now this may be the one characteristic that most defines Illinois, in that it may seem that the state completely lacks hills—the Prairie State is a very apt name for most of the state of Illinois. However, in key areas such as near the Mississippi as it winds around the state, creating the western and southern border, the resulting slopes do make for good grape-growing terrain. Also, southern Illinois' terrain has many undulating hills, ideal for grape growing. It is mainly in these areas that Illinois winemakers who also grow grapes have had success.

With this very brief introduction, I hope you've been able to understand how grape growing and wine making have been able to become so important to Illinois and to its agricultural panorama. The grape grower–winemakers must adapt their techniques to take advantage of Illinois' soil profile while bringing the best worldwide knowhow to bear on producing the best quality wine possible in the Prairie State.

3.
Illinois Grape Varieties

*I*llinois winemakers tend to use hybrids for many reasons we've seen, including Illinois' soil and climate. Hybrid grapes are produced by crossing two or more *Vitis* species. Remember that in other parts of the country or in other parts of the world wine grapes tend to be *Vitis vinifera*. *Vitis labrusca* was North America's indigenous grape. By creating a hybrid of these two, for example, you can bring the flavors of the *Vitis vinifera* grapes into a robust variety that can withstand colder temperatures. *Vitis labrusca* grapes tend to have a candied flavor, while *Vitis riparia* grapes can have herbaceous flavors, but crossing either one with *Vitis vinifera* softens these harsher tones. Hybridization of grapes took off in the early twentieth century as the world tried to avoid another worldwide plague such as phylloxera. Also, winemakers hope to

Baxter's grapes. *Courtesy of Baxter's Vineyards and Winery.*

have grapes with higher yield, for example, or more grapes to the vine, and again hybrid varieties might help them achieve these goals.

Hybridization has a long history. France produced many grape hybrids in the late nineteenth and early twentieth centuries. Subsequently, however, France discouraged planting hybrids. Therefore, hybrid grapes found a new impetus in North America, especially. German scientists also experimented with hybrid grapes. Like many parts of North America, Germany's northerly climate poses problems for ripening grapes and producing consistent quality wine.

Hybrids are cultivars of plants selected for desirable characteristics. In fact, most agriculture today is produced from cultivars, as humans have managed plants to bring out characteristics that make them more useful. Hybrid grapes therefore come from two or more cultivars that have characteristics that winemakers could want—taste and/or resistance to some detrimental condition.

Alto's Chambourcin grapes. *Courtesy of Alto Vineyards.*

Illinois winemakers produce high-quality wines using hybrid grapes. Many of these are crosses of French grape varieties and a *Vitis* genus other than *vinifera*. These cross-pollinated grapes are especially important throughout the Midwest. Two hubs of experimentation with grape hybrids that could thrive in the Midwest tended to be Cornell University in New York and now the University of Minnesota.

In this section, I'll give a very brief definition and some tasting notes for most of the grapes Illinois winemakers produce. So, in alphabetical order, here is an introduction to Illinois grapes:

Baco Noir

This hybrid red grape is a cross of Folle Blanche (*Vitis vinifera*) and an unknown *Vitis riparia* indigenous to North America. It is resistant to many diseases. Baco Noir was grown in France, but in the mid-twentieth century, the European Union limited the use of hybrid grapes. That meant that Baco Noir had to find a new home, in North America. This grape tends to have some smoky flavors.

Brianna

This white, thick-skinned greenish grape is a cross between unknown *Vitis labrusca* and *Vitis riparia* grapes. It can be susceptible to certain type of diseases, but is quite resistant to beetles. Its flavor is semisweet, with some pineapple and grapefruit notes.

Cabernet grapes at Valentino Vineyards.
Courtesy of Valentino Vineyards, Inc. Photo by Rudolph Valentino.

Cabernet Franc

This red grape is one of the most important *Vitis vinifera* grapes in Europe. Some of France's Loire Valley regions use exclusively this grape to make wines, and Cabernet Franc can be a mixing grape in Bordeaux wines and elsewhere. During the second decade of the twenty-first century, Illinois' oenologist was encouraging winemakers to experiment with this grape in Illinois.

Since it thrives in somewhat cooler climates than Cabernet Sauvignon, for example, the experiment yields some interesting results. This grape can have some bell pepper, cassis, violet, and tobacco overtones. I mention this *Vitis vinifera* grape here because Cabernet Franc has established itself as a variety in several vineyards. Other *Vitis vinifera* are still somewhat "rising stars," especially in southern Illinois. I'll mention them at the end of this chapter in one long list.

Catawba

This red hybrid can be used for wine but is used mostly for jellies and juices. It comes from the East Coast and is a cross between *Vitis labrusca* and *Vitis vinifera*. One of the oldest grapes to be used for wine in the United States, it was grown by nurseries for production in the early 1800s. During that time it was the most planted grape in the country. Catawba has a mild berry and somewhat spicy taste, usually.

Cayuga White

This hybrid crosses the Schuyler and Seyval Blanc grapes and was produced at New York's Cornell University. It can have some foxy flavors at times but can be used for good sparkling wines. It can also have pleasant flavors of white flowers.

Chambourcin

These dark red grapes can make excellent wines and are common in Illinois. Joannes Seibel developed them in France in the 1960s. According to the 2011 IGGVA survey, Chambourcin is the most widely planted grape in Illinois, accounting for 12 percent of the state's grape acreage. It tends to produce wine with herbaceous aromas. Chambourcin is moderately hardy, late ripening with large clusters that require thinning. In Illinois these grapes are often used not only for red wines but also for rosé.

Chancellor

This red grape has an undetermined history, a hybrid from several different genuses. It was first produced in Ardèche, France, and came to the United States in the middle of the twentieth century. It produces a medium-bodied wine that is capable of aging. Chancellor grapes have some plum and woody aromas.

Chardonel

This white grape is a cross between the Chardonnay grape and Seyval Blanc. It can produce a full-bodied wine, with some oak flavors, perhaps apple and pear as well. This is one of the most popular white grapes in Illinois, moderately hardy, with midseason ripening loose clusters. It makes a wine with firm acidity.

Concord

We know this grape mostly from unfermented grape juice and jellies. Still, these *Vitis labrusca* grapes can produce wines with a sweet flavor, and they can be used to make a sweet, red wine.

Corot Noir

This hybrid red grape was developed at Cornell in New York for release in 2006, so it is a new variety. A cross between the Seyve Villard grape and the Steuben, this grape is mainly used for blending and has some nice berry and cherry aromas.

Frontenac

The University of Minnesota, a real powerhouse of recent experimentation with wine grapes, produced this hybrid from Landot and cold hardy selections of *Vitis riparia*, the university's first. There is also a white wine version: **Frontenac Gris**. The red grape produces good rosés and port-style wines. It tends to

Chambourcin grapes at Alto Vineyards. *Courtesy of Megan Presnall/IGGVA.*

have aromas of cherry. The white variety has peach, apricot, and some citrus flavors and makes very good dessert and ice wines. These grapes have a high acidity level.

GR 7 / Geneva Red

This grape is a cross between Baco Noir and Buffalo and has had great success in parts of New York state. It is robust and can withstand cold and produces a dark red wine that is a bit lower in acidity than other reds. Many wineries in Illinois are using this grape to great effect, especially as a mixing grape with other varieties. In 2011 this variety was christened **Geneva Red**.

La Crescent

This white hybrid has many parents from a variety of different genuses. It has a fairly intense aroma of apricot, peach, and citrus. It can also have some foxiness from the non-*vinifera* parents. It is excellent for dessert and late harvest wines.

La Crosse

This white grape is a hybrid from several different genuses of grapes. It is thin-skinned, and therefore somewhat prone to leaking. It produces wines with apricot and pear notes, with some floral notes as well. It tends to benefit from malolactic fermentation.

Léon Millot

This grape was born in the early twentieth century in Colmar, Alsace, France. It is a hybrid from the Millardet and Grasser grapes with some Goldriesling, which is a *Vitis vinifera*. The name comes from the winemaker and nursery owner. This red grape is ideal for colder climates but can sometimes have foxy flavors.

Maréchal Foch

This grape was named for the Ferdinand Foch, the chief of the General French Army Staff, hero of World War I, who accepted the German request for armi-stice. It was developed in Alsace, France, and may be a cross between Goldries-ling with *Vitis riparia* grapes. These grapes have good disease resistance. This red grape grows very well in the Midwest and tastes of cherries, strawberries, perhaps sometimes even of raspberries.

Marquette

One of the newest grapes, Marquette already has a great reputation. It has 25 percent of its genetic makeup equivalent to Pinot Noir. These grapes have good disease resistance. Wine from this red grape can resemble *Vitis vinifera* wines.

Muscat

This grape is quite versatile, used for table grapes, raisins, and wine. It is grown around the world and may be the oldest domesticated variety. It is one of the *Vitis vinifera* used in Illinois wine making. There are several subcategories: Muscat Blanc à Petits Grains; Muscat Rose à Petits Grains; Moscatel de Setúbal; Moscatel de Favaios; Muscat of Alexandria; Muscat Ottonel (Muskately); Black Muscat; Orange Muscat; Muscat Crocant; and Moravian Muscat. Each of these

Niagara grapevines at Blue Sky Vineyard. *Courtesy of Blue Sky Vineyard.*

is popular in particular places. In Illinois, Muscat Ottonel does particularly well. Muscat grapes are very popular for sparkling wines, dessert wines, and liqueurs such as brandy, where it imparts a sweet and floral aroma.

Niagara

This is one of the most important *Vitis labrusca* grapes and is the leading green grape (for white wine) in the United States. It does not ship well, so it tends to be used to make wines in areas where it grows well. It has a somewhat foxy flavor but can also have some jasmine-like notes as well as a kind of candied flavor.

Noiret

This hybrid grape was produced at Cornell University for release in 2006, so it is one of the most recent grapes. It was produced from NY 65 and Steuben grapes. It has some notes of green and black pepper, with some mint and raspberry overtones.

Norton

This grape also goes by the name **Cynthiana**. Norton is the oldest cultivated American grape; we have evidence it was already planted to make wine in the early 1800s. Daniel Norton developed the hybrid in 1820. This dark red *Vitis aestivalis* grape produces wines with plum and cherry overtones. It can also produce very good table grapes. It tends to grow small berries, with an intense flavor, although less sweet than Concord grapes, another American variety. These hardy grapes are late ripening and make a wine with high tannins.

Norton grapes at Hickory Ridge Vineyard and Winery. *Author's collection.*

St. Croix

This hybrid grape was produced in 1983 at the University of Minnesota. It makes a deep red wine with lots of fruit aromas such as currants and dried fruit. It is often left to age in oak barrels to give complexity to the wine.

Seyval Blanc grapes at Valentino Vineyards. *Courtesy of Valentino Vineyards, Inc.; photo by Rudolph Valentino.*

St. Pepin

This hybrid grape was created in 1983 from Seyval Blanc and Minnesota 78. This white grape makes an excellent base for blending wines, as well as very good table grapes.

Seyval Blanc

This grape is one of the most planted in the Midwest. This white grape produces wines with grass, hay, and melon aromas. Seyval is a cross of several grape genuses, like so many hybrids. These hardy grapes have midseason ripening but require fruit thinning.

Traminette

This grape was produced in New York from several different grape genuses. This white grape is very popular in Illinois. Wines from Traminette have some spicy notes, like its parent,

Gewürztraminer (or "spicy traminer"), a grape popular in Alsace, France, and in Germany. This grape can produce dry or semidry wines, with some spice and floral aromas. These hardy grapes have large, loose clusters and vigorous vine growth and make a wine with moderate acidity.

Vidal Blanc

This white hybrid grape is a cross between the Ugni Blanc grape and the Rayon d'Or grape developed in the 1930s by Jean Louis Vidal. It can produce high sugar levels even in cold climates. It was produced in France for use in Cognac but has found a home in the United States. It can produce dessert wines, with grapefruit and pineapple aromas. These grapes are moderately hardy, late bud-breaking fruits that require fruit thinning.

Vignoles

This white hybrid, possibly from a Pinot and a Seibel grape, can produce excellent white wines of many different styles, such as dessert, dry, and semidry. It can have aromas of pineapple and apricot in most styles. These hardy, tight-bunched grapes are susceptible to bunch rot and ripen midseason.

Villard

This French hybrid named after the breeder's father-in-law, Victor Villard, comes in several varieties, including the red **Villard Noir**, and the white **Villard Blanc**. Both are crossed from several members of the Villard-Seyval family of grapes and were very popular in France before the European Union mandated

Vignoles grapes. *Courtesy of Megan Presnall/IGGVA.*

Pinot Noir grapes at Valentino Vineyards. *Courtesy of Valentino Vineyards, Inc.; photo by Rudolph Valentino.*

Sangiovese grapes at Valentino Vineyards. *Courtesy of Valentino Vineyards, Inc.; photo by Rudolph Valentino.*

eradication of hybrid grapes. This grape, popular for blending, usually has some citrus characteristics.

Vitis Vinifera: Cabernet Sauvignon, Viognier, Pinot Noir, Petit Verdot, Tannat, Mourvèdre . . .

I've put this category of *Vitis vinifera* grapes all together because it is still rare to have Illinois winemakers experimenting to a great extent with these classic grapes from wine-growing regions all over the world. Cabernet Franc, mentioned earlier, is the one with which most experimentation has gone forward. However, perhaps in the future, more experimentation will take place with traditional *Vitis vinifera* grapes. As I wrote this book, only a few vintners mentioned they were growing these grapes. The University of Minnesota, for example, continues to experiment heavily with new varieties suited to northern climates. Certainly Illinois will benefit from the results of these experiments. After all, as climate patterns change, Illinois' relationship to growing grapes may change along with it.

4.
Bottles, Stoppers, and Labels

*W*ine is a delicate commodity. Its flavor and balance can be ruined if it is stored in the wrong container. For that reason, wine containers have evolved little for centuries. Illinois wines come in packages that mirror trends in the rest of the world.

CONTAINERS

Most Illinois wines still come in the traditional glass containers. Illinois law mandates wineries use a new bottle for each bottle of wine produced. Glass has existed since about 2500 B.C. The Romans probably invented glassblowing to shape ornamental dishes that are still found in archeological digs. The material needed to be made thin but strong enough to withstand the pressure of wine without breaking. Around 1700, probably in England, a thicker, colored glass was made into vessels: the wine bottle was born.

Today wine still comes primarily in bottles, although new types of containers are arriving every day. "Chateau cardboard," or boxed wines, are now fairly prevalent. "Box" wines are even rated in important wine magazines such as the *Wine Spectator*, whereas until well into the new millennium they were considered inferior. It's not really a bad way to keep wine fresh, since these boxes are lined

Bottles ready to fill. *Author's collection.*

with a bladder pack that collapses as wine is consumed. The primary enemy of wine is oxygen, so keeping oxygen away from wine helps keep "off" smells out.

Plastic bottles are also increasing in popularity. They are more lightweight than glass and thus cost less to transport. Every penny saved on transport helps keep wine prices in line. The newer types of plastic are said not to impart plastic flavor to the wine. That has always been the primary hindrance to using plastic; it has a smell that can contaminate good food or beverage. However, as technology evolves and improves, we are sure to find even newer ways to bring wine to the table.

STOPPERS

With stoppers the situation becomes a bit more difficult. For centuries corks were the norm. The cork tree, primarily found in Portugal and Spain, provided a solution for stopping wine. The thick bark gives a porous, but impermeable seal. Corks let just enough air enter the bottle to keep the wine aging without spoiling. They keep wine away from harmful oxygen and are easy to extract without getting splinters in the wine (cork shards left by a dry cork are not dangerous, they are just messy to drink).

Now, however, wine stoppers are more varied. Wines are often sealed with synthetic corks, or even with screw caps. The change came because many wines seemed off, like eggs, sherry, or vinegar. It turned out they were infected, often through natural cork, with 2,4,6-trichloranisole (or TCA) or sometimes 2,4,6-tribromoanisole (or TBA), two substances that can be found in wineries and that negatively affect wine if they come in contact with it. A vintner cannot

August Hill Winery cork. *Courtesy of Elliot Weisenberg.*

afford to have the reputation of his or her wine ruined when a consumer finds it tainted.

To address these problems, plastic corks were developed. The screw top, long used for inferior wine or soda pop, is also increasingly popular. Made of metal and completely airtight, it is not affected by taint with TCA or TBA.

Neither the plastic cork nor the screw cap has passed the test of time. We are not certain if wines that need years of aging will benefit from these closures. Right now we know that wines aged with real corks do continue to age in the bottle. This is beneficial because red wines tend to soften with minute quantities of oxygen coming into contact with the wine over a period of many years. This allows the harsher tannins to precipitate out of the wine (and create sediment in the bottom of the bottle, for example), making the wine taste softer.

The screw cap is, however, gaining a following. Some studies from 2010 note that screw caps did well with wines aged ten years. But the jury is still out on longer aging. Most often Illinois winemakers produce bottles meant for consumption within a short time from when they are bought. (In fact, statistics show the overwhelming majority of wine worldwide is consumed within a year of purchase.) This is one reason why Illinois wine can readily use plastic corks, screw caps, or real corks. You'll find all three when you buy Illinois wines. Don't be put off by the screw caps, thinking the wine in that bottle is necessarily inferior. Remember, virtually all the delicious wines of New Zealand, for example, even the most prestigious, now use screw caps. For those Illinois wines meant to be put in your cellar, none as of now claims the wine can age for decades. So enjoy the wine no matter what the closure!

LABELS

For most consumers, the most important piece of information on the label may be grape names. Many are easy, and we recognize them immediately: Merlot, Cabernet Sauvignon, and Chardonnay are well known all over the world. Blends of several grapes may include grape names on the back or front labels, but usually the blend will have a creative name rather than the names of the grapes.

The wine label has evolved. Even ancient Greek and Egyptian jars had information describing the wine. Once the glass bottle came into use, labels included the name of the wine, perhaps the year, and sometimes the grower or shipper. Labels provide primary information to the consumer, but they can also reveal the creativity of the winemaker. While certain areas of the world, in Europe for example, have fairly strict limitations on what information a label can contain, in the United States winemakers can be more expansive. Some basic information, however, is still common: the year (vintage); the name of the wine (with details as specific as necessary to tell you the quality level of the wine); the AVA (American Viticultural Area); if the wine was made organically or biodynamically; individual vineyard designation; grape variety; estate bottled or reserve designation. Back labels will often tell consumers about the types of oak barrel, how long the wine was aged, and something about the vintner or the area (if it is unique) and the shipper, grower, or vintner, depending on the wine. There's an indication of the volume of liquid in the bottle and the alcohol content also, either on the front or the back label, required by law. Also required by law is the disclaimer about consuming alcohol as potentially detrimental to health. In the United States, the grape may be listed on the label if at least 75 percent of what's in the bottle is made from that grape.

The Bureau of Alcohol, Tobacco, Firearms, and Explosives (ATF) regulates wine labels in the United States. They considered requiring much more information than it currently does (calories, serving sizes, carbohydrates, and so

Plainview Vineyard label. *Courtesy of Plainview Vineyard.*

on) but decided against it given the backlash from people opposed to alcohol, who said that adding this information would lead consumers to think of wine as a nutritious beverage. Debate still surrounds adding more information on labels, which many vintners find an unnecessary intrusion.

Illinois wine labels vary from the simple and descriptive to the artistic. In preparing this book, I was told by some winemakers that they enlisted friends and relatives to create original artwork for their labels. Others worked with marketing consultants. Still others stuck to images for their labels that represent central characteristics of the name of the winery or the landscape surrounding the vineyard. Since Illinois wines are mainly produced using hybrid grapes whose names don't tend to be universally recognized, Illinois winemakers often bottle using fanciful names rather than listing the grapes on the label. In each profile in the following part of the book, you will find many of these wine names. Almost universally, the Illinois winemakers invested quite a bit of energy and pride in their labels, knowing they would be the "front door" to the wines contained in the bottles.

So Illinois wines and their packaging tend to be somewhat traditional. However, winemakers do emphasize closures that seem to protect wines destined for fairly timely consumption. While the cork closure is definitely still in existence, plastic and screw caps hold a strong position among Illinois winemakers. Labels provide essential information, but also give an introduction to a winemaker's creativity. In all areas, Illinois wines want to show up on your table looking as pleasant to the eye as they taste in your mouth.

5.
Purchasing, Storing, and Tasting Illinois Wine

*H*opefully you're interested in this book because you want to taste Illinois wine during your tour of Illinois. To describe wines as you enjoy them, you need to develop vocabulary. Most of the vocabulary of wine consists of adjectives and nouns describing odors. Many of the nouns are, in fact, common: *blackberry*, *violets*, *amber* (*white*), and so on.

Adjectives used to describe wines tend to be of sensations, tastes, or smells, since appreciating wines is one of the most satisfying sensory activities.

Some drinkers find it difficult to identify wine aromas. It seems difficult to home in on the exact smells a wine may impart. You may ask yourself, What is that somewhat tangy smell—lemon? Tomatoes? You can tell there is something beyond the smell of alcohol but it's mysterious—maybe mushrooms? Identifying exact smells can be one of the most frustrating aspects of wine tasting as you begin your journey. It also tends to be one of the most potentially intimidating. If everyone else in the tasting room identifies honeysuckle in the white wine, but to you it "smells like wine," you may think your future as a wine enthusiast is doomed.

Fear not. Wine tasting, identifying the hundreds of potential smells a wine can emit, begins with developing your olfactory memory. You should start to associate wine smells with things they remind you of, someone you know, or a previous experience. Try to focus on what you remember when you think of that person or event. For example, if you eat lots of red meat, notice how the meat smells a bit like iron. Red meat indeed has iron-containing compounds, so there's no surprise that you can identify that smell when you eat the meat. If you try to concentrate as you smell things, and make associations, you should be able to become an expert wine smeller!

When you are smelling wines, some aromas fall into "main categories," into which fall subcategories and special aromas. For example, in the "woody" category, you may be able to distinguish burnt wood from resinous wood. You

Hogg Hollow wineglass. *Courtesy of Hogg Hollow Winery, LLC* .

Owl Creek dessert wine. *Courtesy of Owl Creek Vineyard.*

may be able to further distinguish cedar and oak in the resinous wood, or coffee in the burnt wood.

You may want to get a copy of the "tasting wheel," first developed at the University of California, Davis. It can help you find adjectives and nouns to associate with smells. Illinois wine, as we've seen, tends to be produced from hybrid grapes. This means in terms of tasting they will mainly contain a mixture of smells from the *Vitis vinifera* grape that bore the hybrid. Hybrids thrive in Illinois, and in much of the Midwest, because they bring the hearty, resistant characteristics of *Vitis labrusca* (mostly) to mix with the flavor characteristic of *Vitis vinifera* (Cabernet Sauvignon, Sauvignon Blanc, and so on). The grape chapter of this book contains most of the grapes used in Illinois, along with some aroma characteristics. Remember, the flavors listed here are only a few common traits that many wine drinkers can discern in the wines. You may be able to identify an entirely different set of smells and tastes. That remains one of the most pleasant aspects of wine tasting: "owning" a wine by defining its taste for yourself.

A WORD ABOUT PURCHASING ILLINOIS WINES

We're entering into a legal area that for many is difficult to comprehend. Strict laws governing the transport and sale of wines, especially over state lines, have been with us since the end of Prohibition. Many Chicagoans wonder why Illinois wines are not more easily available in the biggest market for wine in the whole state.

Lavender Crest's winery tour. *Courtesy of Lavender Crest Winery.*

In 2008 new legislation modified the way wines can be shipped. The Internet has opened up wine sales and therefore has made wine laws that restrict the sale and transport of wine across state lines impractical. New legislation allows Illinois winemakers to ship wines to other states.

Shipping and distributing wines can be very expensive. It requires a special license, which allows a winery to ship twelve cases of wine per adult resident per year. The license cost depends on the size of the winery. There is also an exception for smaller wineries to self-distribute wines. Before applying for the license, the winery must prove it has been granted federal label/bottle approval and that it has a bonded warehouse space. Of course this is above and beyond the various manufacturer applications involved in producing alcohol. Given the myriad forms involved, some Illinois wineries have decided that it is not cost-effective to distribute their wines unless the market gives more of a guarantee of being favorable to Illinois wine. Small wineries in many cases have decided not to ship but to sell wines only on the premises.

In Chicago there are other distribution laws that make it very difficult, and costly, to penetrate the Chicago market. Certain distributors have been able to have very broad interests in distributing liquor in the city.

However, shipping and delivering Illinois wine to Chicago may be getting somewhat easier. *Midwest Wine Press* reported in 2012 that despite weak demand, a few Chicago outlets have Illinois wine. Macy's on State Street carries twenty regional wines. Also, Mariano's Fresh Market carries fourteen regional

Silver Moon Winery's buffet. *Courtesy of Silver Moon Winery.*

wines.[1] Also, several restaurants in the Chicago area are beginning to offer Illinois wines to diners along with wines from other parts of the country and world.

This increased availability could be part of the "locavore" movement, where locally produced foods and consumables have a privileged reputation with certain consumers. It may also be a product of image. Illinois wine has lagged behind California, Oregon, Washington state, and others. Marketing has much to do with the popularity of products. Still, there is hope that as Illinois wines gain in reputation they will also be easier to find.

Illinois wine styles are changing. I mentioned earlier that some ambitious winemakers are purposely moving away from what they call their grandfathers' sweet wines for which Illinois was known and instead are focusing on international dry wine styles.

So the best way to get Illinois wine is to go to a winery yourself. Short of that, ask the winery to ship to you. That could prove costly, but if you are determined it could be a great option. Or you can try to find these wines in your local area restaurants and stores.

Already now, certain larger wineries in Illinois provide delivery services. Others make their wines available in retail stores, usually near the location of the winery. Some state directly that they can no longer ship wine, presumably because the costs associated with shipping and delivery have become prohibitive.

---

1. Michael Sean Comerford, "Regional Wine Fighting Its Way into Chicago," *Midwest Wine Press*, October 25, 2012, midwestwinepress.com/2012/10/25/chicago-wine-sales-market.

TAKING CARE OF YOUR WINE

You've purchased your Illinois wine and would now like to keep it around to share with friends the next time they come over. You need some guidelines for storing wines. First, remember that Illinois wines, at least in the early years of the new millennium, are not made for extremely long cellaring after you buy them. In general, hybrid grapes are usually used to make wines for consumption not long after they are produced. That's ideal because Illinois wines are indeed often meant to be consumed young.

Below are a few tips for how to treat your wines as well as possible from the time you bring them home to when you drink and share with friends.

- Keep your wines at constant temperature.
- Don't put wine near a furnace or an air conditioning unit.
- Keep wines out of the kitchen, unless you use a special temperature-controlled unit for wines. You can store wines in the fridge for brief periods of time, especially white wines. Kitchen (and bathroom) temperatures fluctuate too much because of hot water faucets and appliances, so keeping wines in the kitchen may damage them.
- Do put your wines in a cool, dry basement. If your basement floods, forget it.
- Do store wine somewhere in the inside of the house, ideally in the corner of a room, against an internal wall, away from windows, where there is too much exposure to temperature fluctuations.
- Wines closed with real corks should be stored on their sides.

It's now time to taste your Illinois wine. You've treated it well and invited your friends, and you're ready to serve. What elements of the wine will you look for? There are five taste categories that come through

Hailey's Winery and Vineyard storage display. *Courtesy of Hailey's Winery, Ltd.*

Grafton Winery's terrace. *Courtesy of Grafton Winery and Brewhaus.*

tongues: saltiness, sweetness, sourness, bitterness, and *umami*. (Umami is a Japanese concept to describe the taste of glutamate, an amino acid found in many foods. We can find it in mushrooms or in tomatoes.)

According to the Court of the Master Sommeliers, wines can be identified by color, smell, and taste. Those, then, are the components we'll want to try to find in the wines.

- *See*: Look for the color, and look for off signs such as rings. For example, in general, Chancellor, Cabernet Franc, and Chambourcin will be a denser red as compared to Pinot Noir, a more cherry-red color. Whites can vary from almost clear to golden yellow (the latter for Rieslings). Dessert wines may even be orange or a burnt-brown color, almost like caramel. Old wines can be identified by brown or orange tints in red wines, darker yellow or brown in white wines.
- *Swirl*: This is where you swish the liquid in your glass so the wine gets in contact with even more oxygen. This allows you to really taste as much of the flavor as possible.
- *Smell*: We know this is most important. Really get your nose in the glass; really work with it to see what's there.
- *Savor*: This is where you can actually drink the wine. Taste for things like acidity level, especially for a white, and for tannins if you have a red.[2]

---

2. Reproduced in part from Clara Orban, *Wine Lessons: Ten Questions to Guide Your Appreciation of Wine* (Dubuque, Iowa: Kendall Hunt Publishing, 2012), 183–84.

WINE AND FOOD PAIRINGS

One of the most pleasant aspects of sharing wines with friends involves drinking it with a meal. Illinois wines come in so many varieties that you are certain to find ones that work well with virtually any meals. Most wineries in Illinois provide hints on how their wines pair with food. Ask for suggestions if you have a particular dinner in mind.

In general, when selecting pairings, you should take into consideration the weight of the food. A heavy wine will kill a light dish, and a light wine will die in the presence of a heavy dish. A Chancellor (medium heavy) with cream-sauced fish (light) would not work well; neither would a Vignoles (light) with a steak (heavy).

You will also want to take into consideration the spiciness or sweetness of the food or wine. A very sweet wine (late harvest, port, dessert) will kill savory food and should be saved for after dinner. Those wines will be ideal with salty cheeses such as blue, but they also go very well with cakes and desserts. Likewise, a spicy dish will work only with certain types of wines (sweeter wines work well, for example). Some foods usually don't go well with wine: dishes made with vinegar, such as salad dressing for example, but they are relatively few. In general, sparkling wines go well with salty or creamy food.

Wine tasting at Forsee Vineyards. *Courtesy of Forsee Vineyards and Winery.*

Stronger meats such as grilled red meats tend to go well with heavier red wines such as Chambourcin, and the like. Fish tends to go well with lighter white wines. Pork, veal and chicken adapt to the type of sauce in which they are prepared. In general, you'll want to pair the wine to the sauce rather than the meat.

Cheese of all types tends to go well with wine. Which ones depend on the wines. For example, try a goat cheese with a light Chardonel, and a blue cheese with a port-style wine. Port wines are fortified with brandy, added to stop the fermentation from completely converting the sugar to alcohol. These wines are therefore sweeter than most wines and higher in alcohol (usually about 18–20 percent, rather than 7–14 percent for table wines). These sweet wines counteract the tanginess of the blue cheese.

Now we get to what for some is the best part: dessert! Illinois wines tend to go very well with certain types of dessert. Many Illinois winemakers produce dessert wines that are ideally suited to sweet treats. Dessert wines have higher levels of sugar in the wine and are specifically produced to capitalize on their sweetness. You may see some of the following when you are looking for dessert wines:

- *Late harvest*: This means the grapes were allowed to remain on the vines after the normal harvest date for that particular year. That would mean the grapes had more time to create sugar and are therefore sweeter than they normally would be. This sweetness transfers to the bottle. These wines are more difficult to make because they involve a risk. If the weather turns bad before the winemaker can harvest, he or she may lose those grapes. Late harvest wines have become popular in Illinois because many of the hybrid grapes used lend themselves very well to this style.
- *Port*: As we mentioned above, port-style wines are fortified by adding brandy to the fermentation, which kills the yeasts before the sugar can completely convert to alcohol. Since brandy is so much more alcoholic than wine, that means fortified wines tend to be sweeter and higher

Server at Blue Sky Vineyard. *Courtesy of Blue Sky Vineyard.*

Lincoln Heritage Winery's courtyard. *Courtesy of Lincoln Heritage Winery.*

in alcohol. As we said, port-style wines tend to go well with blue cheese, but they are also ideal with chocolate—dark, milk, and white.

- *Ice wines*: This unique style originated in Germany, another very cold climate for growing grapes that, nonetheless, has been doing so successfully for millennia. Grapes for ice wines are allowed to remain on the vines until the first frost. They are picked frozen, and as they melt, the water, which was frozen, will leak out, concentrating the sugary juice in the liquid that remains to be processed. These wines tend to be sweet and excellent with all kinds of pastries and almond cookies, for example, where the slight bitterness of the almonds contrasts perfectly with the wine's sweetness.
- *Sparkling wines*: One of the exciting developments in Illinois is the increasing interest in producing sparkling wines. With their higher acidity levels, many Illinois hybrids are ideal for sparkling wines. Some Illinois winemakers have even begun creating sparkling wines here using the "méthode traditionnelle," the laborious but exacting method for creating sparkling wines first developed in the Champagne region of France. Many producers use alternate methods for adding bubbles, such as the Charmat method, or adding carbon dioxide. In the traditional method, the key to bubbles involves allowing wines to undergo a second fermentation in the bottle by reintroducing yeast after the wine has undergone primary fermentation. For Charmat, second fermentation takes place in the tank and the wine is subsequently bottled under pressure. Whatever the method, sparkling wines from Illinois will prove to be very interesting new additions to Illinois' wine panorama.

Many Illinois wines have lighter characteristics than wines from exclusively *Vitis vinifera* grapes. Some people tend to think of them as wines with more "sweetness." This may not always be the case; people sometimes confuse fruitiness—that is the obvious fruit characteristics of a grape (aroma of raspberry, for example)—with sweetness (residual sugar in the wine). Illinois wines do tend to be somewhat lighter, and perhaps fruitier or even a bit sweeter than wines from warmer climates. These qualities, though, make these wines often ideal with cuisines that are hard to pair with wine. Asian or Mexican cuisines tend to have strong spices that often overwhelm wines. One of the "tips" of pairing wines and food, however, is that sweeter and lighter wines stand up well to spicier cuisine. You might want to try some of these Illinois wines when you have Chinese or Mexican food. This is where you'll want to consult the winemakers or their wine list. Some of the bottles that maker produces may be great with meats, or pasta, or may be ideal for spicy food. Remember Illinois wines in the context of these exotic food options.

In all cases, enjoy the wines from the great wineries featured on the following pages!

6.
Illinois Winery Profiles by Region

*I*n compiling this book, I worked from the website and official lists compiled by the IGGVA. For that reason, if a winery is not on their list, you may not find it in these pages. The list was complete as of this writing, summer 2013. New wineries may have opened their doors in the meantime; others may have closed. Also, the IGGVA lists multiple tasting room addresses for a winery as individual listings. For the purposes of this book, I have listed each winery once. In the following profiles I have emphasized the grape wines the wineries produce. If a winery only produces wine from other fruits, I have listed these in the profile. In all cases, we are only able to include a selection of what's offered by each winery.

Every effort was made to give an accurate picture of a winery, through questionnaires, phone calls, and websites. In some cases, I was forced to edit information because it made the profile too long. In others, I had little information at my disposal. In all cases, I thank the winemakers of Illinois and the IGGVA for their help, their enthusiasm, and their knowledge as I compiled this list. Before visiting the wineries in this book, call or go online to check the latest information about location, closing hours, and so on.

A great way to visit wineries is to have someone else do the driving. Consider taking a tour with Evanston Cellars in northern Illinois and other midwestern states ([847] 864-0199) dileep@evanstoncellars.com with SI Tours in southern Illinois (info@sitours.net / [618] 985-6953), or with other tour operators in this growing field.

I hope this helps you discover and enjoy the wines of Illinois.

NORTHERN *Region*

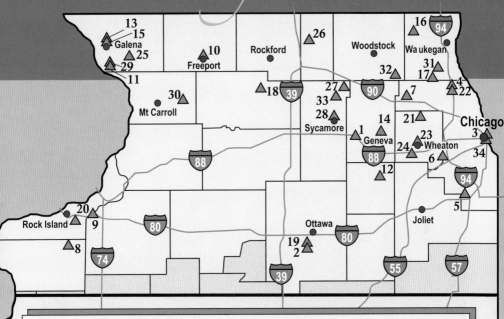

Northern Region Wineries

1. Acquaviva Winery
2. August Hill Winery/Illinois Sparkling Co.
3. City Winery
4. Cooper's Hawk Winery and Restaurant
5. Cooper's Hawk Winery and Restaurant
6. Cooper's Hawk Winery and Restaurant
7. Cooper's Hawk Winery and Restaurant
8. Creekside Inn and Seasonal Terrace Tasting Room
9. Creekside Vineyards, Winery, and Inn
10. Famous Fossil Vineyard and Winery
11. Fergedaboudit Vineyard and Winery
12. Fox Valley Winery, Inc.
13. Galena Cellars
14. Galena Cellars Tasting Room
15. Galena Cellars, Winery, and Vineyard
16. Glunz Family Winery and Cellars
17. Glunz Family Winery and Cellars Tasting Room

18. Hailey's Winery, Ltd.
19. Illinois River Winery
20. Lavendar Crest Winery
21. Lynfred Winery
22. Lynfred Winery
23. Lynfred Winery's Tasting deVine
24. Lynfred Winery's Tasting deVine
25. Massbach Ridge Winery
26. McEachran Homestead Winery
27. Prairie on State Wine Cellars
28. Prairie State Winery
29. Rocky Waters Vineyard and Winery, Inc.
30. Silver Moon Winery
31. Valentino Vineyards, Inc.
32. Village Vintner Winery and Brewery
33. Waterman Winery and Vineyard, Inc.
34. Wild Blossom Meadery and Winery

Acquaviva Winery. *Courtesy of Midwest Wine Press.*

ACQUAVIVA WINERY

Owners

The Brandonisio family

History

This family-owned forty-acre estate includes a twenty-thousand-square-foot facility with tasting bar, Neapolitan pizza oven, private-event space, and beautiful architecture. The fine art in the winery comes from world-renowned artist Andre Zabela (whose works have been showcased in Sweden, Finland, Japan, and many other countries). Vito Brandonisio's grandfather operated a small winery in Acquaviva delle Fonti, Bari, Italy, and continued the tradition once he arrived in the United States. The estate's name is in homage to his homeland: "living water."

Sample of Grapes Grown

Some of the grapes grown here are Brianna, Chardonel, Frontenac, Maréchal Foch, and Prairie Star.

Winery

Tasting room hours, for the Maple Park location are Tuesday–Thursday, 11 AM–9 PM; Friday–Saturday, 11 AM–10 PM; Sunday, NOON–8 PM.

SAMPLE OF WINES PRODUCED AT THIS AWARD-WINNING WINERY

Wine	Style	Grapes
Red		
Piacere	Dry red	Chancellor blend
Vitino	Dry red	Maréchal Foch
White		
Donna Mia	Dry	White blend
Prairie Star	Semidry	Prairie Star
Bianco Bello	Semisweet	Chardonel

Contact and Directions

47W 614 Route 38, Maple Park, IL 60151. (630) 365-0333.

AUGUST HILL WINERY

Owners

Mark Wenzel and Teri Wenzel

History

The Wenzels have operated the vineyard and winery, as well as the August Hill Winery Tasting Room in historic downtown Utica, just minutes from Starved Rock State Park, since beginning their project in 2004. August Hill Winery was founded by Sean Ginocchio and Mark and Teri Wenzel. Mark and Sean, early grade-school friends, began their winery days in 2000, when Mark became the guardian of a portion of his family's farmland.

Standing on the land once tilled by his grandfather, August (Augie) Engelhaupt, Mark felt his passion for farming reignite. He remembered as a child watching his grandfather Augie carefully tend the scenic piece of land overlooking the Illinois River valley. Mark wanted to capture Augie's insatiable passion and share it with others and began studying wine making.

Although Sean is no longer involved in the daily operations, he and his family continue to support August Hill Winery, helping out with special events and corporate sales. Sean's wife, Tara, continues to create her paintings that are included on labels and marketing materials and are shown in the tasting room gallery.

SAMPLE OF GRAPES GROWN

Grape Name	Acreage
Cabernet Franc	1.75
Chambourcin	2
Chardonel	1
Frontenac	2
Frontenac Gris	1.5
Golden Muscat	1.25
Léon Millot	0.5
Maréchal Foch	2.5
St. Pepin	2
Seyval Blanc	2.5
Traminette	3
Vignoles	2

Winery

Tasting room hours:
Friday–Saturday, 10 AM–8 PM;
Sunday, 11 AM–5 PM;
Monday–Thursday, 10 AM–5 PM.
Seating accommodations indoors and on three-season outdoor patio.

Other

The tasting room August Hill Wines carries not only wine but also other handcrafted creations, including paintings, sculpture, glass art, and more from a select group of featured artists. Other items for sale include wine gift baskets, wine accessories, glassware, gourmet chocolates, and artisan cheeses.

Contact and Directions

106 Mill Street, Utica, IL 61373. (815) 667-5211. info@augusthillwinery.com. In downtown Utica, close to Starved Rock State Park.

August Hill Winery wines. *Courtesy of August Hill Winery.*

SAMPLE OF WINES PRODUCED AT THIS AWARD-WINNING WINERY

Wine	Style	Grapes
Red		
Cabernet Franc	Dry	96% Cabernet Franc, 4% Frontenac
Ginocchio	Dry	Sangiovese, Cabernet Franc, Frontenac, Maréchal Foch
Hieland Red	Dry	Frontenac
Okoye	Dry	Maréchal Foch, Chambourcin, Frontenac
Berlyn	Semidry	Frontenac, Chambourcin
Trapolino	Semisweet	Maréchal Foch, Frontenac, Léon Millot
White		
Chardonel	Dry	95% Chardonel, 5% Vignoles
Seyval Blanc	Semidry	93% Seyval Blanc, 7% St. Pepin
Traminette	Semidry	Traminette
Vignoles	Semidry	75% Vignoles, 25% Golden Muscat
Sweet William	Semisweet	60% Muscat, 40% Seyval Blanc
Niagara	Sweet	Niagara
Other		
Desert Rose	Semidry rosé	75% Maréchal Foch, 25% Frontenac
Muscato	Slightly carbonated, sweet	Golden Muscat
Almond Infusion	Carbonated, sweet	Seyval Blanc, Golden Muscat
Raspberry Infusion	Carbonated, sweet	Seyval Blanc, Golden Muscat
Mardi Gras	Carbonated, sweet blush	Catawba

ILLINOIS SPARKLING CO.

August Hill's Sparkling Wine Production Company

Owners
Mark Wenzel and Teri Wenzel

History
Years ago Mark and Teri Wenzel, owners of August Hill Winery, became fascinated with Champagne. When Mark, the winemaker for August Hill, realized

Illinois Sparkling Co. wines, Franken's and Stereo. *Courtesy of Illinois Sparkling Co.*

that Illinois was a region primed to produce world-class sparkling wine grapes, he began experimenting with sparkling wine. After years of research, trials, and some great advice from Champagne producers, Illinois Sparkling Co. was born in 2004.

Illinois Sparkling Co. is an independent craft winery obsessed with making exceptional sparkling wine using the traditional method. The grapes used are 100 percent Illinois grown, and each wine is handcrafted at the winery in Peru, Illinois.

SAMPLE OF GRAPES GROWN

Grape Name	Acreage
Chambourcin	2
Frontenac	2
Frontenac Gris	1.5
La Crescent	1.5
Maréchal Foch	2.5
St. Pepin	2
Seyval Blanc	2.5
Other experimental	0.66

Winery

Tasting room hours:
Friday–Saturday, 10 AM–8 PM;
Sunday, 11 AM–5 PM;
Monday–Thursday, 10 AM–5 PM.
Seating accommodations indoors and on three-season outdoor patio.

Other

Other items for sale: the ISC Flight (three two-ounce pours plus nosh plate), artwork by local artists, wine gifts and accessories, glassware.

Contact and Directions

106 Mill Street, Utica, IL 61373. (815) 667-5211. PopCulture@IllinoisSparkling Co.com. In downtown Utica, close to Starved Rock State Park.

SAMPLE OF WINES PRODUCED AT THIS AWARD-WINNING WINERY

Wine	Style	Grapes
Franken's	Traditional method Brut sparkling wine	Chambourcin
I.S.C. Brut	Traditional method Brut sparkling wine	St. Pepin, Seyval Blanc
Heirloom	Traditional method Brut sparkling rosé	Maréchal Foch
Stereo	Traditional method sec sparkling wine	La Crescent, Frontenac Gris
Dollface	Traditional method demi-sec sparkling rosé	Frontenac

CITY WINERY

Owner
Michael Dorf, Founder and CEO

History
The first City Winery began in New York as a space to combine wine and music. Customers could make their own wine, buy wine and food on the premises, and listen to music at one of many events hosted in the space. The second "City Winery" opened in Chicago in 2011 and is even bigger than the New York location. It was the first operational winery in the city limits. Budding winemakers in the Chicago winery can use grapes sourced from many areas of the country and of the world. By the time of this printing, City Winery Chicago may be offering Illinois grapes as well. The space hosts many concerts, private parties, and other events.

Sample of Grapes Grown
The winery does not grow its own grapes.

Winery
Tasting room hours: Daily, 5 PM–MIDNIGHT, and Sunday brunch, 10:30 AM–2 PM. Patio hours: Monday–Friday, 4 PM–10 PM, and Saturday–Sunday, NOON–10 PM. Concert dining hours: dinner, 6 PM–MIDNIGHT (drinks served until 1 AM), and Sunday Klezmer Brunch, 11 AM–2 PM (doors open at 10 AM; ticket required for entry).

Sample of Wines Served
Many national and international wines of all types are served in the facility.

Robert Kowal of City Winery with his tanks and kegs. *Courtesy of Midwest Wine Press.*

Other

Event space can be rented. City Winery also offers a donation program for charity events. Please contact them for details. They have a thirty-thousand-square-foot facility, 175-seat restaurant, three-hundred-seat concert hall, thirty-seat private barrel dining room, and a large private garden/courtyard. The modular space can accommodate many types of occasions.

Contact and Directions

1200 W. Randolph Street Chicago, IL 60607. (312) 733-9463. Chicago@city winery.com. About 2 miles west of Lake Shore Drive in Chicago.

Cooper's Hawk Winery and Restaurants display at Oak Park's Uncork Illinois. *Courtesy of Elliot Weisenberg.*

COOPER'S HAWK WINERY AND RESTAURANTS

Owner
Tim McEnery, Founder and CEO

History
Cooper's Hawk represents a concept of wineries and restaurants where the wines are produced off-site. Cooper's Hawk in Orland Park, Illinois, opened in 2005, and there are five other Illinois locations. They also include locations outside Illinois. Their restaurant serves food and wines in their "own private winery." The Cooper's Hawk concept includes dining room, bar, private barrel aging room, and "Napa-style" tasting room.

Sample of Grapes Grown
The winery does not grow its own grapes.

Winery
Tasting room information varies by location.

Sample of Wines Served at This Award-Winning Winery
The winery serves wines from international grapes such as Pinot Noir and Sangiovese.

Contact and Directions

Cooper's Hawk has several Illinois locations including Arlington Heights, 789 Algonquin Road, 60005. (847) 981-0900 / Burr Ridge, 510 Village Center Drive, 60527. (630) 887-0123 / Naperville, 1740 Freedom Road, 60563. (630) 245-8000 / Orland Park, 15690 S. Harlem, 60462. (708) 633-0200 / South Barrington, 100 W. Higgins Road, 60010. (847) 836-9463 / Wheeling, 583 N. Milwaukee Avenue, 60090. (847) 215-1200.

⸺ ❧ ⸺

CREEKSIDE VINEYARDS, WINERY, AND INN

Owners

John Mital and Jennifer Mital

History

John and Jennifer, the original owners, purchased Creekside Vineyards in 2006 and released their first vintage in 2010 after their first harvest. They have called the present location home since 2012. They are recent vintners, but their enthusiasm and foundation in science have already attracted attention for their wines. Creekside's tasting room rests in a newly renovated 1940s building, which has been alternately used for various purposes. Their second location boasts a Seasonal Terrace and Inn and is considered one of the highlights of the Quad Cities area.

Creekside Vineyards, Winery, and Inn. *Courtesy of Creekside Vineyards, Winery, and Inn.*

SAMPLE OF GRAPES GROWN

Grape Name	Acreage
La Crescent	1
La Crosse	2
Marquette	1

Winery

Tasting room hours: Year-round inside and seasonal terrace seating May–October.

SAMPLE OF WINES PRODUCED AT THIS AWARD-WINNING WINERY

Wine	Style	Grapes
Red		
Country Road	Dry	Chambourcin
First Kiss	Dry	Maréchal Foch
Old Bull	Dry	Marquette
Rock Island Red	Dry	Frontenac
White		
Creekside White	Semidry	La Crosse
Front Porch	Semidry	Traminette
Sundaze	Semidry	Seyval Blanc
Moonbeam	Semisweet	La Crescent
Crooked Owl	Semisweet	La Crosse
Other		
Blushing Bonnie	Blush	Chambourcin

Other

Creekside Vineyards, Winery, and Inn offers a year-round bed-and-breakfast, seasonal Terrace Wine Tastings, and live music.

Contact and Directions

Seasonal Terrace and Inn: 7505 120th Avenue, Coal Valley, IL 61240. Winery and Tasting Room: 1667 US Highway 67, Preemption, IL 61276. (309) 787-9463. info@creeksidevineyards.com. Less than 5 miles from the Quad Cities International Airport, they welcome visitors. For the Seasonal Terrace, take I-74 to Route 150, then go south on West Third Street to 120th Avenue. For the Winery and Tasting Room, go 9 miles south of Milan, Illinois, on Highway 67.

FAMOUS FOSSIL VINEYARD AND WINERY

Owner
Ken Rosmann

History
Famous Fossil vineyard was planted in 2004, and the winery opened October 2008. The name Famous Fossil was inspired by the many fossils emerging from the ground as the vineyard was established. Some of these fossils are displayed in the tasting room, where you may sample wines, watch wine being made, or enjoy wine at barrel tables. In warm weather, seating is available on the deck overlooking the vineyard and the rolling hills of northern Illinois. Events are held all year long.

The winery, built in 2008, was designed as a "green" building, including ten- to twelve-inch structured insulated panels, triple pane windows, passive solar, underground cooling rooms, a high velocity heating/cooling system with an on-demand water heater, Energy Star appliances, and the use of formaldehyde-free and low VOC materials and products and recycled products whenever possible. The vineyard is managed using sustainable farming practices. Naturally occurring yeasts are used with slow, cool fermentation.

Sample of Grapes Grown
Grapes include Brianna, Frontenac, King of the North, La Crescent, La Crosse, Marquette, Petite Ami, Petite Jewell, Prairie Star, and St. Croix. Famous Fossil wines use grape varieties developed specifically for the cold climate of the

Famous Fossil Vineyard and Winery's winery entrance. *Author's collection.*

Famous Fossil Vineyard and Winery's outdoor seating. *Author's collection.*

upper Midwest. They also have several experimental varieties they are testing for private breeders.

Winery
Tasting room hours: open year-round daily. Seating: 50.

SAMPLE OF WINES PRODUCED AT THIS AWARD-WINNING WINERY

Wine	Style	Grapes
Red		
Fossil Creek Red	Dry	Blend
Fossil Rock Red	Dry	Frontenac
Bedrock Red	Semidry	Blend
Heritage	Semisweet	Blend
White		
Crescent Moon White	Dry to Semidry	La Crescent
Fossil Rock White	Semidry	Blend
Traminette	Semidry	Traminette
Vignoles	Semisweet	Vignoles
Other		
Over the Moon	Dry sparkling	La Crescent

Other
The tasting room features handcrafted gift and home items made by local artisans. The winery uses local foods for its events and private parties.

Contact and Directions
395 W. Cedarville Road, Freeport, IL 61032. (815) 563-4665. www.famous fossilwinery.com. Highway 20 to Galena, exit 26 toward Cedarville, Illinois.

Fergedaboudit Vineyard and Winery's tasting room. *Courtesy of Fergedaboudit Vineyard and Winery.*

FERGEDABOUDIT VINEYARD AND WINERY

Owner
Rosario Bruno

History
The family purchased the land in 1999 and in 2000 planted 1,300 grape plants. Previously, this forty-six-acre plot was primarily used for growing alfalfa and provided pasture for grazing. They built the winery building in 2001 and harvested the first crop of grapes in 2004. Wine making, however, was a family tradition. Rosario started making wine with some friends in their Chicago cellar, combining old world and new world techniques. Hailing from a Sicilian family, Rosario often used the phrase "Ferged Aboud It" when describing events of his life—his catchphrase became the winery's name.

SAMPLE OF GRAPES GROWN

Grape Name	Acreage
Cabernet Franc	0.25
Frontenac	0.125
GR 7	0.25
Léon Millot	1
Maréchal Foch	0.25
Marquette	0.5
NY 72	0.125
St. Vincent	0.125
Traminette	0.125

Winery
Tasting room hours:
April–November,
Thursday–Sunday, 11 AM–5 PM.
Seating: 30.

SAMPLE OF WINES PRODUCED AT THIS AWARD-WINNING WINERY

Wine	Style	Grapes
Red		
Frontenac	Dry	Frontenac
Léon Millot	Dry	Léon Millot
Maréchal Foch	Dry	Maréchal Foch
Vino di Pappi	Dry	Cabernet Franc, St. Vincent
Zinfandel	Dry	California Zinfandel
White		
Charcato	Sweet	California Chardonnay blend

Other
Souvenirs, glasses, and T-shirts are on sale in the winery.

Contact and Directions
4595 Speer Road, Hanover, IL 61041. (815) 591-2126. winemaker@fergedaboudit.com. From Chicago, take I-90 to Route 39, Route 20 bypass. Go west on Route 20 to Route 84, then go south 4½ miles to Speer Road to the vineyard. From there it is 1½ miles to the tasting room.

FOX VALLEY WINERY, INC.

Owner
Richard A. Faltz

History
The winery began in August 2000 after a long period of intense research. In the 1990s research, planning, and development of the vineyards and winery (two separate locations) kept the family busy. Especially crucial was studying a possible grape-growing venture in Illinois. The family ultimately planted the vineyard, against most of their advisors' professional advice because of the risk involved.

Early in 2003 they found a permanent winery location, but it took two years to change the zoning, get local approvals and licensing, and begin operations—all this only to learn that the site in the township location was "dry" and they could not sell wine by the glass or bottle because of a township vote in the 1930s prohibiting it!

Still, this perseverance paid off, and Fox Valley Winery now welcomes visitors to its beautiful location.

Faltz Family Vineyard at Fox Valley Winery. *Courtesy of Fox Valley Winery, Inc.*

SAMPLE OF GRAPES GROWN

Grape Name	Acreage
Chardonnay	1
Corot Noir	1.25
Frontenac	1
Landot Noir	1.25
Noiret	1.25
Pinot Noir	1
St. Pepin	0.5
Traminette	1

Winery

Tasting room hours:
Monday–Thursday, NOON–6 PM;
Friday–Saturday, 11 AM–7 PM;
Sunday, 11 AM–5 PM.
Seating: 75.

SAMPLE OF WINES PRODUCED AT THIS AWARD-WINNING WINERY

Wine	Style	Grapes
Red		
Chambourcin	Dry	Chambourcin
Sec Noir	Dry	Cabernet Franc, Lemberger
White		
Sec Blanc	Dry	Seyval Blanc, Vidal Blanc
Traminette	Semidry	Traminette
Riesling	Semisweet	Riesling
Other		
Dry Rosé	Dry	Frontenac, Vidal Blanc

Other

They specialize in marketing, displaying, and sales of individual artisan creations from local artists in their tasting room. The French Country tasting room and Garden Patio is available for parties and special events. They specialize in small-lot batches developed from single vineyard locations, and single varietal bottling to demonstrate Illinois terroir-driven wine styles.

Contact and Directions

5600 US Route 34, Oswego, IL 60543. (630) 554-0404. Karen.thompson@fox valleywinery.com, richard.faltz@foxvalleywinery.com, oswego@foxvalleywinery .com. On the west side of Oswego at 5600 US Route 34. Go 8 miles south of I-88, ½ mile east of Orchard Road, ½ mile west of Illinois Route 31.

<hr />

GALENA CELLARS, WINERY, AND VINEYARD

Owners

Scott Lawlor and Christine Lawlor-White

History

Galena Cellars is one of the most established and well-known wineries in the Midwest. They offer forty different wines in three locations. Their work and enthusiasm for wine now spans three generations. Enjoy their wines while relaxing on their spacious deck. They are part of the Mississippi River Valley AVA, the largest grape-growing appellation in the world. The vineyard stretches for many acres that produce sixty thousand gallons of wine per year.

Winery and barn of Galena Cellars, Winery, and Vineyard. *Courtesy of Megan Presnall/IGGVA.*

SAMPLE OF GRAPES GROWN

Grape Name	Acreage
Frontenac	1
La Crosse	2
Maréchal Foch	1
St. Croix	2

Winery

Tasting room hours vary by location but include May–October, Sunday–Thursday, 11 AM–6 PM, and Friday–Saturday 11 AM–8 PM; April–November, Friday and Saturday, 11 AM–6 PM, and Sunday, 11 AM–5 PM; and December–March, Saturday, 11 AM–5 PM.

SAMPLE OF WINES PRODUCED AT THIS AWARD-WINNING WINERY

Wine	Style	Grapes
Red		
Eric the Red	Dry	Maréchal Foch
Vincent Red	Dry	St. Croix
White		
Brit White	Dry	Chardonel
Daffodil	Semidry	La Crosse
Illinois Traminette	Semidry	Traminette
Other		
Vineyard Rose	Semidry	St. Croix
Chocolate Port	Sweet	Frontenac
Frontenac Port	Sweet	Frontenac

Other

The gift shop sells wine-related gift items.

Contact and Directions

Three locations at 515 S. Main Street, Galena, IL 61036. (800) 397-9463 / 4746 N. Ford Road, Galena, IL 61036. (815) 777-3235 / Dodson Place, 477 S. Third Street, Geneva, IL 61034. (630) 232-9463. rob@galenacellars.com.

GLUNZ FAMILY WINERY AND CELLARS

Owner

Joe Glunz Jr.

History

They are producers of small-batch fortified wines, table wines, and seasonal wines from grapes as well as other fruit. The family has been purveyors and producers of wine since 1992. Their cellar master, Ciprioano, will be glad to escort visitors through the cellar.

Sample of Grapes Grown

The winery does not grow its own grapes.

Winery

Tasting room hours:
Tuesday–Saturday, 10 AM–6 PM, and Sunday, NOON–5 PM.
Closed Monday.

Other

The owner and cellar master will show visitors around the cellar.

Contact and Directions

888 E. Belvidere Road, #107, Grayslake, IL 60030. (847) 548-9463. winetogo@gfwc.com; info@gfwc.com.

Glunz Family Winery and Cellars' tasting room. *Courtesy of Megan Presnall/IGGVA.*

SAMPLE OF WINES PRODUCED

Wine	Style	Grapes
Red		
Everyday Red	Dry	Blend
White		
Everyday White	Dry	Blend
Other		
Angelica	Fortified	Blend
Vintage Port	Fortified	Blend
Sangria		Blend
May Wine		

HAILEY'S WINERY LTD.

Owners

Cheryl Spana (formerly Hailey) and Ginger Baerenwald

History

The winery, owned by Jim and Cheryl Hailey, opened in April 2009. As the winery grew, at one point there were twenty-three fermentation tanks in operation. Sadly, Jim passed away in early 2011. Ginger joined Cheryl as co-owner of Hailey's in October 2011. Together they have been busy with production,

Hailey's Winery Ltd. bottles. *Courtesy of Hailey's Winery Ltd.*

creating new wines, and striving to provide a warm, inviting atmosphere for wine exploration. Their raspberry wine, Ruby Sipper, was released in 2012, and new Norton and Chardonel varieties were released midyear in 2013.

Sample of Grapes Grown
The winery does not grow its own grapes.

Winery
Tasting room hours: Tuesday–Thursday, NOON–6 PM; Friday–Saturday, NOON–7 PM. (Weekend hours vary for music events.) Seating: 45–50.

SAMPLE OF WINES PRODUCED AT THIS AWARD-WINNING WINERY

Wine	Style	Grapes/Fruit
Red		
Chambourcin	Dry	Chambourcin
Just Norton	Dry	Norton
Road Trip Red	Dry	Noiret
Rocking Chair Red	Semisweet	Chambourcin, Concord
White		
Chardonel	Dry	Chardonel
Niagara	Dry	Niagara
Seyval Blanc	Dry	Seyval Blanc
Timeless White	Dry	Chardonel
Girl's Night White	Semisweet	White blend
Sweet Niagara	Sweet	Niagara

Other

The shop sells cheeses, sausage, homemade bread, chocolates, beer selections, and gift items. In addition, the winery hosts casual gatherings, live music, and private events.

Contact and Directions

114 S. Franklin Street, Box 478, Byron, IL 61010. (815) 234-2220. The winery is just off Route 2/72 in the middle of Byron. Franklin Street intersects Route 72 just west of the new library. Haileys@haileyswinery.com.

❧

ILLINOIS RIVER WINERY

Owner

Gregg Kane

History

The winery was founded in 2002 when Gregg Kane started Starved Rock Vineyards.

The family has agricultural roots, and they decided to establish the winery near Starved Rock after having visited often. They began planting grapes in the 1990s. The primary vineyard of twelve acres is at the historic St. Bede Abbey. This Benedictine monastery continues a tradition dating back to the first centuries of Christianity, when St. Benedict founded the order. The abbey, next to the winery, provides a beautiful stopover in Illinois wine country.

Illinois River Winery. *Author's collection.*

SAMPLE OF GRAPES GROWN

Grape Name	Acreage
Cayuga White	1.5
Concord	1
Niagara	0.5
Riesling	1.5
Traminette	1
Valvin Muscat	4.5

Winery

Tasting room hours:
Sunday–Thursday, 10 AM–6 PM;
Friday–Saturday, 10 AM–8 PM.

Other

The winery offers an "artist in residence" program to promote Illinois art. They provide accommodations in the winery apartment so artists can create their work.

SAMPLE OF WINES PRODUCED

Wine	Style	Grapes
Red		
Cabernet Franc	Dry	Cabernet Franc
Norton	Dry	Norton
Lil Ole Truck	Sweet	Concord
White		
Cayuga White	Semisweet	Cayuga White
Other		
Pink Side of the Moon	Blush	Cabernet, Merlot, Frontenac
Port of Utica	Dessert	Concord

Contact and Directions

723 S. Clark Street, North Utica, IL 61373. (815) 667-4012. The winery is across the river from Starved Rock State Park.

LAVENDER CREST WINERY

Owners

Martha Rittmueller and Wilbert Rittmueller

History

The Rittmuellers are the original owners and opened the winery in 2004. Their winery is near the Quad Cities, an ideal location near the Mississippi. The name was chosen as a reminder of childhood experiences Martha had with her grandmother and a lovely lavender field. For their wines, they use eighteen to twenty tons of grapes from five growers, although they also grow grapes themselves. Their winery location allows for easy access on its nine acres near I-80.

Lavender Crest Winery's patio. *Courtesy of Lavender Crest Winery.*

SAMPLE OF GRAPES GROWN

Grape Name	Acreage
Concord	2 rows
Maréchal Foch	8 rows
Niagara	8 rows

Winery

Tasting room hours: 11 AM–5 PM.
Seating: tasting room, 75;
banquet room, 275; patio, 100.

SAMPLE OF WINES PRODUCED AT THIS AWARD-WINNING WINERY

Wine	Style	Grapes
Red		
Crimson	Dry	Frontenac
Miche Sepi	Dry	Cabernet, Maréchal Foch
Ritt's Reserve	Dry	Chambourcin
Colona Red	Semidry	Merlot, Maréchal Foch
1836	Semidry	Chancellor
Red Velvet	Semisweet	Maréchal Foch
Chocolate Love	Sweet	Maréchal Foch, Essence of Dark Chocolate
Foxy	Sweet	Concord
White		
Catch of the Day	Dry	Chardonel
Traminette	Dry	Traminette
Majestic	Semidry	Vignoles
Colona White	Semisweet	Seyval Blanc
Faithful Friends	Semisweet	Seyval Blanc
Beaches	Sweet	Niagara
Sweet Temptation	Sweet	Traminette, Muscat

Other
Items for sale include gifts. The winery serves lunch and dinner on Friday. The banquet room is available for weddings, special events, and corporate affairs.

Contact and Directions
5401 US Highway 6, Colona, IL 61241. (309) 949-2565. info@lavendercrest.com. Near I-80 and the Mississippi River.

LYNFRED WINERY

Owners
The Koehler family

History
The winery opened October 14, 1979. The concept of Lynfred Winery came from "two crazy people," as they themselves described it. It was entirely a creation of the love and ingenuity of Fred and Lynn Koehler.

The Koehlers were pioneers in the Illinois wine industry, but their road was not easy. Getting the business of a winery in Roselle, Illinois, off the ground took quite a while. Starting in a historic house that was originally built by the Hattendorf family in 1912, the Koehlers went to work restoring the house and organizing a cellar to expand their "hobby" into a business. The one acre of land Lynfred currently occupies was originally owned by Colonel Roselle Hough, after whom the city was named. The leaded stained-glass windows and oak floors and

Lynfred Winery celebrated its thirty-third anniversary in 2013. The winery has come a long way from the original tasting room opened in 1979, the oldest continually operating winery in Illinois. Lynfred has now expanded into a twenty-four-thousand-square-foot facility. The expanded facility, which is connected by a vaulted barrel-aging tunnel, has increased wine production and storage facilities. The new facility's oaken tasting room and gift shop are accented by many of the highlights of the "old" house, including beautiful stained glass, burgundy velvet walls, and wonderful oaken stairwells and floors. On the top floor are four bed-and-breakfast suites. Fred Koehler passed away in July of 2011, but his vision of Lynfred Winery lives on. Lynfred Winery produces more varieties than any other winery in the United States, under one brand, with over eighty different wines annually.

moldings were restored to their original state. The cellar walls, which are more than eighteen inches thick, provide ideal temperature control for aging wines.

Sample of Grapes Grown
The winery does not grow its own grapes.

Winery
Tasting room hours: open daily, 10 AM–7 PM.

SAMPLE OF WINES PRODUCED AT THIS AWARD-WINNING WINERY

Wine	Style	Grapes
Red		
Cabernet Sauvignon	Dry	Cabernet Sauvignon
Merlot	Dry	Merlot
White		
Chardonnay	Dry	Chardonnay
Pinot Grigio	Dry	Pinot Grigio

Other
Wine and Cheese Pairings, available in their VIP Room on Thursday and Friday evenings 4 PM–6 PM and Saturday and Sunday afternoons (1 PM–6 PM), include three wines, three cheeses, and fresh breadsticks. Epicurean Experience includes three wines paired with six appetizers, available on Saturday afternoons at 1 PM and 4 PM.

Lynfred Winery barrel. *Courtesy of Megan Presnall/IGGVA.*

Contact and Directions

15 South Roselle Road, Roselle, IL 60172. (630) 529-9463. They have several stores: Tasting deVine–Wheaton. (630) 752-9463 / Tasting deVine Cellars–Naperville. (630) 420-9463 / Lynfred Winery–Wheeling. (847) 229-9463. wine info@lynfredwinery.com.

MASSBACH RIDGE WINERY

Owner
Peggy Harmston

History
The owner moved back to the ancestral family farm and researched grapes and wine before starting what is currently eighteen acres of vineyard and a six-thousand-gallon winery. The family enjoys making a premium local wine and sharing their beautiful countryside with others. The cozy winery has a unique décor that will welcome visitors. They have been crafting estate-grown wines since 2003 on eighteen rolling acres of vineyard and countryside.

SAMPLE OF GRAPES GROWN

Grape Name	Acreage
Concord	1
Frontenac	3
La Crosse	1
Maréchal Foch	12
St. Pepin	4
Vignoles	2

Winery
Tasting room hours:
open daily, 11 AM–5 PM.
Galena location:
Sunday–Thursday, 11 AM–5 PM,
Friday–Saturday, 11 AM–8 PM.

SAMPLE OF WINES PRODUCED AT THIS AWARD-WINNING WINERY

Wine	Style	Grapes
Red		
Massbach Reserve	Dry	Maréchal Foch, Frontenac
Träumen	Sweet	Frontenac
White		
Windsong White	Dry	St. Pepin
St. Pepin	Semidry	St. Pepin
Seyval	Semidry	Seyval Blanc
Vignoles	Semidry	Vignoles

Massbach Ridge Winery. *Courtesy of Megan Presnall/IGGVA.*

Other

The winery offers a comfortable place to enjoy a glass of wine.

Contact and Directions

Two locations: 8837 S. Massbach Road, Elizabeth, IL 61028; and 117 S. Main Street, Galena, IL 61036. (815) 291-6700. Massbachridge@bhawk.net.

MCEACHRAN HOMESTEAD WINERY

Owner

Herbert Greenlee

History

The only winery in Boone County, Illinois, McEachran's vineyard was planted in 2006, while the winery opened in 2010. McEachran Homestead was settled in 1857 by John McEachran, the owner's great-great-grandfather. He immigrated to northern Illinois from Scotland and settled in what was then known as the Argyle Scottish Settlement. McEachran Homestead is officially recognized by the state of Illinois as a Sesquicentennial Farm. The original farm of 160 acres has been expanded to 285 acres with corn and soybeans as the main crops. Eleven acres are dedicated to nineteen varieties of grapes, raspberries, and fruit trees, all of which are meticulously tended, then handcrafted into cold-climate grape and fruit wines.

McEachran Homestead Winery's entrance. *Courtesy of McEachran Homestead Winery.*

Sample of Grapes Grown

Some of the grapes grown on their two acres are Brianna, Concord, Delaware, Edelweiss, Frontenac, La Crescent, La Crosse, Léon Millot, Maréchal Foch, and Niagara.

Winery

Tasting room hours: Wednesday–Saturday, 10 AM–5 PM. Seating: lower-level tasting room, 20; upper-level restored hay loft, 60.

SAMPLE OF WINES PRODUCED

Wine	Style	Grapes
Red		
Ae Fond Kiss	Sweet	Niagara, Reliance
Frontenac	Sweet	Frontenac
Maréchal Foch	Sweet	Maréchal Foch
White		
La Crescent	Sweet	La Crescent
St. Pepin	Sweet	St. Pepin
Other		
Steuben	Blush	Steuben

Other

The wine selection rotates seasonally. Fruit wines—red raspberry and strawberry rhubarb, made from fruit grown on their farm; cranberry, made from Wisconsin-grown fruit; cherry, made from Door County cherries; blueberry, made from Michigan fruit. They also sell wine slushies, a combination of wine and fruit juice, chilled and perfect for summer.

Contact and Directions

1917 Wyman School Road, Caledonia, IL 61011. (815) 978-5120. info@mceachran homestead.com. Ten miles northeast of Rockford, 6 miles northeast of I-90–Route 173 interchange.

PRAIRIE STATE WINERY

Owner
Rick Mamoser

History

Rick Mamoser and Maria Mamoser opened Prairie State Winery in 1999 after several years as high school teachers. The winery in Genoa has expanded several times and now occupies four buildings in downtown. They recently opened a second tasting room in Sycamore called Prairie on State. The winery resembles an old-time country store. With their emphasis on locally produced merchandise and wines, they consider themselves part of the "keep it local" and "locavore" movements. Their philosophy: "Think Globally, Drink Locally." Rick won "winemaker of the year" several times.

Sample of Grapes Grown

The winery does not grow its own grapes.

Winery

Tasting room hours: Genoa, Monday–Thursday NOON–5 PM, Friday 10 AM–6 PM, Saturday 10 AM–5 PM, and Sunday, NOON –5 PM. Sycamore, Monday–Tuesday 11 AM–5 PM, Wednesday–Thursday 11 AM–7 PM, Friday 11 AM–8 PM, Saturday 11 AM–8 PM, and Sunday NOON–5 PM. Seating: Genoa, 80; Sycamore, 50.

Other

Wine accessories, wine racks, cheeses, and gourmet food items are for sale in the winery. They offer wines exclusive to each location. They also sell fruit wines, sangria, specialty wines like "snap" flavored with ginger, and sparkling wines. The winery hosts events as well.

Prairie State Winery's tasting room. *Courtesy of Dileep Gangolli.*

SAMPLE OF WINES PRODUCED AT THIS AWARD-WINNING WINERY

Wine	Style	Grapes
Red		
Cabernet Franc	Dry	Cabernet Franc
Nawt'n	Dry	Norton
Prairie Red	Semidry	Chambourcin
State Red	Semidry	Maréchal Foch
White		
Oak Savanna	Dry	Chardonel
Prairie White	Semidry	Seyval Blanc
Kishwaukee Blue	Semisweet	Vidal Blanc, St. Pepin
Lacrescent	Semisweet	La Crescent

Contact and Directions

Genoa: 217 W. Main Street, 60135. Sycamore: 322 W. State Street, 60178. (815) 991-5266. info@prairiestatewine.com. Genoa: near I-72 and Route 20. Sycamore: near I-64 and Route 23. The newest location is Prairie on State Cellars, 322 W. State Street, Sycamore, IL 60172. (815) 991-5266.

ROCKY WATERS VINEYARD AND WINERY, INC.

Owners
Jared Spahn and Phyllis Spahn

History
Jared Spahn and Phyllis Spahn bought 112 acres in Hanover, Illinois, in 1994, although they are both natives of Iowa. The land has fast-running creeks, one of the reasons for the name "rocky." Rocky Waters sold grapes to Galena Cellars in 2001 and 2002 and to Wollersheim Winery in 2003 and 2004. In 2008 the commercial winery was opened as their twenty-five acres of red and white varietals became mature enough to totally support the winery.

SAMPLE OF GRAPES GROWN, TWENTY-FIVE ACRES TOTAL

Grape Name	Acreage
La Crosse	2
Léon Millot	3.5
Maréchal Foch	13
St. Croix	3.5
St. Pepin	3

Winery
Tasting room hours:
Monday–Saturday, 10 AM–6 PM;
Sunday, 11 AM–4 PM.

Contact and Directions
2003 W. Hanover Road, Hanover, IL 61041. (815) 591-9706. jcs@rockywaters.net or kds@rockywaters.net

Rocky Waters Vineyard and Winery, Inc. *Courtesy of Celestino Ruffini.*

SAMPLE OF WINES PRODUCED AT THIS AWARD-WINNING WINERY

Wine	Style	Grapes
Red		
Homestead Red	Dry	Maréchal Foch
Tower Red	Dry	Maréchal Foch
White		
Prairie Gold White	Dry	St. Pepin, La Crosse
Lakeside White	Semidry	St. Pepin, La Crosse
Log Cabin White	Semisweet	St. Pepin, La Crosse
Other		
Wild Turkey Blush	Semidry	Maréchal Foch
Cedar Lake Blush	Semisweet	Maréchal Foch
Highland Blush	Semisweet	St. Croix
Meadow Blush	Semisweet	Léon Millot

SILVER MOON WINERY

Silver Moon Winery's tasting room. *Courtesy of Silver Moon Winery.*

Owners

Ron Enzenbacher and Kathi Enzenbacher

History

Silver Moon Winery began on a fifty-five-acre site in northwestern Carroll County, close to Lake Carroll and just outside Lanark. The family purchased the lands, being used for grazing cattle, in 2004. The first year, they worked on amending the soil by planting soy, as the cattle grazed.

Over six thousand vines were then planted on twenty acres of gently rolling hillsides. They also planted an orchard of five hundred fruit trees and five hundred fruit bushes on an adjoining ten-acre site. Each vintage has seen gains and losses in the vineyard. Cold climate vines such as Frontenac and Maréchal Foch are maturing with time. They have replanted where they have lost other less hardy vines: it is still a very young vineyard. The tasting room was opened in April 2010.

Sample of Grapes Grown

Some of the grapes grown on a total of twenty acres include Einset, Frontenac, La Crosse, Léon Millot, Maréchal Foch, NY 76, Reliance, Rubina, Sabrevois, St. Croix, St. Pepin, and Valvin Muscat.

Winery

Tasting room hours: September–December and April–May, Saturday NOON–5 PM, Sunday NOON–3 PM. Summer (June–August), Saturday NOON–6 pm, Sunday NOON–4 PM.

SAMPLE OF WINES PRODUCED

Wine	Style	Grapes
Red		
Red Velvet	Dry	Blend
White		
Chardonel	Dry	Chardonel
Moonlight White	Dry	Blend
Midwest Traminette	Semisweet	Traminette
Other		
Twilight	Blush	Blend

Other

They offer a "New Moon Tasting," which changes each month, pairing four wines with specialty bites of complementary foods. They also feature exclusive Illinois Red Velvet Cheddar cheese made locally with their Red Velvet Wine. They also offer cheese plates made with locally produced cheeses. The tasting room features an exclusive selection of imported extra virgin olive oils and balsamic vinegars. They also have a large selection of wine related items, glasses, and gifts and will gladly put together a custom basket.

Contact and Directions

21305 Zier Road, Lanark, IL 61046. (815) 493-6888. www.silvermoonwineryinc.com. Take IL 72 west to Zier Road.

VALENTINO VINEYARDS, INC.

Owner
Rudolph V. Di Tommaso

History
The winery estate was established by the current owner in 1995. The winery opened in 2001. Valentino Vineyards grows over five thousand vines—French hybrid, American hybrid, *Vitis vinifera* (twenty varieties). All wines are barrel aged, nonfiltered, and low sulfite.

Sample of Grapes Grown
On its twenty acres, Valentino Vineyards and Winery produces grapes that include Bianca, Brianna, Chardonnay, Frontenac, Maréchal Foch, Marquette, Pino Grigio, St. Croix, Sangiovese, Seyval Blanc, and Vignoles.

Winery
Tasting room hours: April–December, Monday–Thursday, by appointment; Friday, 5 PM–7 PM; Saturday, 11 AM–5 PM; Sunday, NOON–4 PM. Seating: 65.

SAMPLE OF WINES PRODUCED AT THIS AWARD-WINNING WINERY

Wine	Style	Grapes
Red		
Cabernet Franc	Dry	Cabernet Franc
DeChaunac	Dry	DeChaunac
Maréchal Foch	Dry	DeChaunac, Maréchal Foch
Signature Red	Dry	Blend
White		
Bianca Ice	Semisweet	Bianca
Bianca Late Harvest	Sweet	Bianca
Other		
Red port	Sweet	Blend
White port	Sweet	Blend

Other
Cheese and wine items are for sale in the winery.

Contact and Directions
5175 Aptakisic Road, Long Grove, IL 60047. (847) 634-2831. valentinowinery@aol.com. From Chicago, take I-94 north to the Deerfield Road exit, then turn left (west) onto Deerfield Road. Turn right onto Milwaukee Avenue, then left onto Aptakisic Road.

Valentino in vineyard. *Courtesy of Valentino Vineyards, Inc.; photo by Rudolph Valentino.*

☙

THE VILLAGE VINTNER WINERY AND BREWERY

Owner
Steve Boyer

History
This new location offers a wood-fired pizza oven, a full-service bar, and a tasting bar. Handcrafted beers, made on the premises, are also a specialty. The wines are handcrafted from grapes sourced worldwide. The winery closed for about six months before opening in the new location. This is only one of three brewery-wineries in Illinois.

Sample of Grapes Grown
The winery does not grow its own grapes.

Winery
Tasting room hours: open daily, Monday, 5 PM; Tuesday–Thursday, 11 AM–10 PM; Friday–Saturday, 11 AM–11:30 PM; Sunday, NOON–9 PM.

SAMPLE OF WINES PRODUCED

Wine	Style	Grapes
Red		
Barbera	Dry	Barbera
Tuscan Red	Dry	Brunello
White		
Chenin Blanc	Dry	Chenin Blanc
Viognier	Dry	Viognier

Other

The winery also serves craft beers made on the premises.

Contact and Directions

2380 Esplanade Drive, Algonquin, IL 60102. (847) 658-4900. info@thevillage vintner.com. Take Randall Road north off I-90.

The Village Vintner Winery and Brewery's seating area and barrels. *Author's collection.*

The Village Vintner Winery and Brewery's new winery building. *Author's collection.*

❦

WATERMAN WINERY AND VINEYARD, INC.

Owners
Terrie, Alexa, and Trisha Tuntland; Clem Stiely; Anne Stiely

History
The current owners produced the winery's first planting in 1998. The business was subsequently incorporated in 2000. The vineyard is on the family farm in DeKalb County, Illinois. Being hilly and well drained, the vineyard is visually appealing. There is good "isolation" and a stand of pine trees to the west of the vineyards, making it a great location to grow grapes.

Guests enjoy wine tasting in a casual agricultural setting. The winery, vineyard, and farm have received the 2010 "sustainability award" from the state of Illinois and the DeKalb County Soil and Water Conservation Award. There are forty different grape varietals in the vineyard.

Owners of Waterman Winery and their winery display. *Courtesy of Midwest Wine Press.*

Growing their own grapes and fermenting and bottling on-site also allows for full control of this regional wine operation. Within an hour after harvesting, the grapes are crushed and destemmed, and fermentation begins. No long over-the-road transportation is necessary.

SAMPLE OF GRAPES GROWN

Grape Name	Acreage
Concord	1
Frontenac	2
Frontenac Gris	0.5
GR 7	0.5
La Crescent	2
Léon Millot	2
Maréchal Foch	2
Niagara	2

Winery

Tasting room hours:
April–December,
Saturday–Sunday, NOON–4 PM;
also by appointment.
Seating: over 12.

SAMPLE OF WINES PRODUCED

Wine	Style	Grapes
Red		
Royal Red	Dry	Maréchal Foch, Léon Millot
Waterman Red	Dry	Frontenac
Sunset Table	Medium dry	Blend
Sweet Sunset	Sweet	Blend
White		
Wine Dog	Dry	La Crescent
La Crescent	Sweet	La Crescent
DeKalb County Niagara	Sweet	Niagara
Blush	Medium sweet	Concord

Other

They host events at the winery such as wine tasting.

Contact and Directions

11582 Waterman Road, Waterman, IL 60556. (815) 264-3268. sunsetwines@sunsetwines.com. The winery is 10 miles south of DeKalb.

Greg Fischer of Wild Blossom Meadery and Winery. *Courtesy of Midwest Wine Press.*

WILD BLOSSOM MEADERY AND WINERY

Owner
Greg Fisher, winemaker and beekeeper

History
This winery was actually founded to produce mead, an alcoholic beverage made from honey. Wild Blossom is Chicago's first winery, on the Far South Side. Furthermore, it is the only meadery on the Northern Illinois Wine Trail.

Sample of Grapes Grown
This winery does not grow its own grapes.

Winery
Tasting room hours vary.

Sample of Wines Produced at This Award-Winning Winery
The winery produces several types of grape wine with red and white grapes. Its primary production involves mead, an ancient honey-based alcoholic beverage.

Contact and Directions
10033 S. Western Avenue, Chicago, IL 60643. (773) 233-7579. wildblossom @bevart.com. From I-55 take Western Avenue south; or from I-57, take Western Avenue north.

CENTRAL
Region

55

39

57

△4
Toulon

△5
Peoria ●

74

△13
7 △
● Bloomington

△2
Nauvoo

△6
Carthage

14 △

155

55

74

1 △
△15
△9
Champaign

Danville ●

57

10
△   △11
Quincy ●

△8
Mt. Sterling

3 △
Lincoln ●

55

72
Decatur ●

74

72
Springfield ● △12

57

Central Region Wineries

1. Alto Vineyards Champaign
2. Baxter's Vineyards and Winery
3. Hill Prairie Winery
4. Indian Creek Vineyard
5. Kickapoo Creek Winery
6. Lake Hill Winery and Banquet Hall
7. Mackinaw Valley Vineyard and Winery
8. Ridge View Winery, LLC
9. Sleepy Creek Vineyards
10. Spirit Knob Winery
11. The Village Vineyard and Winery
12. Walnut Street Winery
13. White Oak Vineyards
14. Willett's Winery and Cellar
15. Wyldewood Cellars Winery

ALTO VINEYARDS CHAMPAIGN

For contact information about this winery, see the Alto Vineyards entry in the "Southern Region" section of this chapter or go to http://www.altovineyards.net/news_champaign.htm.

BAXTER'S VINEYARDS AND WINERY

Owners
Brenda Logan and Kelly Logan

History
Baxter's Vineyard is a small family-owned business in Nauvoo, Illinois, the first winery in Illinois. Emile Baxter established the winery in 1857. He came to Nauvoo in 1855 to join an Icarian community, which soon after, however, disbanded. The Baxters moved to the east coast, but then decided to move back and soon after established the vineyard. In 1880 the family purchased the Wasserzierher Wine Cellar, built in 1863, which already contained eighteen casks. The family continued to create wine through the succeeding decades. Now, more than a century later, Kelly Logan is the fifth generation of family winemakers.

SAMPLE OF GRAPES GROWN

Grape Name	Acreage
Catawba	2
Cayuga White	0.5
Chambourcin	0.5
Concord	8
Corot Noir	0.5
Frontenac	0.5
Niagara	2
Noiret	1
Norton	3
Vidal and other varieties	0.1 each

Winery
Tasting room hours: Monday–Saturday, 9 AM–5 PM; January–March, Sunday, NOON–5 PM; April–December, Sunday, 10 AM–5 PM, for self-guided tours and wine tastings. Seating: 20.

Other
They also sell nonalcoholic grape juices.

Contact and Directions
2010 E. Parley Street, Nauvoo, IL 62354. baxters@frontiernet.net. (217) 453-2528. Eleven blocks off Highway 96 going through Nauvoo State Park on Parley Street.

Baxter's Vineyards and Winery wines. *Courtesy of Baxter's Vineyards and Winery.*

SAMPLE OF WINES PRODUCED AT THIS AWARD-WINNING WINERY

Wine	Style	Grapes
Red		
Riverbend Red	Dry	Noiret, Corot Noir
Icarian Red	Semidry	Concord, Vidal Blanc
Nauvoo Red	Semidry	Noiret
Classic Catawba	Semisweet	Catawba
Classic Concord	Sweet	Concord
White		
Captain's White	Dry	Vidal Blanc, Traminette

HILL PRAIRIE WINERY

Owner
Mark Lounsberry

History
Before Hill Prairie came into existence as a vineyard and winery, it was a typical grain and livestock farm. The family's ancestors traveled to Illinois eight generations ago from Pony Hollow, New York, in 1832. Matthew Lounsberry brought his family here, and the following year his father, Matthew Sr., his brother Jonathan, and his two sisters and their families came: thirty-two people in all.

Hill Prairie Winery. *Courtesy of Megan Presnall/IGGVA.*

They all lived in one log cabin west of present-day Oakford for two months until more homes could be built. They were among the first settlers before Oakford came into existence in 1872. In 1887 some of them moved to the location of Hill Prairie, built a farmstead, and worked the land with large draft horses. The fifth generation, now teenagers, works in the vineyard.

*T*he present-day site of the vineyard is surrounded by native Illinois prairie grasses, preserved to look much like the original Illinois prairie that greeted the first settlers. Since that time, with the advent of the steel plow, the natural prairie slowly disappeared. It was plowed under to make way for the cultivation of grain and forage crops. Until recently, steep knobs or hills, often located in wooded areas or near river bluffs, were the only remnants of prairies. They are usually small parcels of land, sometimes only a few square feet on top of a hill called "hill prairies." In recent times the seeds from the plants have been reproduced commercially, and programs have been put in place to restore large areas of prairie plants. This vineyard and surrounding area is one of the restored prairies.

Sometime near 1911, J. T. Lounsberry built the structure that stands today as Hill Prairie Winery. Its original purpose was to house draft horses and work animals. The upper loft was used to hold hay. Horses remained a part of the farm and were kept in this barn until the 1980s. Homer Lounsberry was the last horseman to ply his trade here and was well known for his knowledge and love of horses.

SAMPLE OF GRAPES GROWN

Grape Name	Acreage
Chardonel	4
Frontenac	2
Frontenac Gris	1
St. Croix	1
Vignoles	1

Winery

Tasting room hours: Monday–Saturday, 11 AM–5 PM; Sunday, NOON–5 PM. Indoor and outdoor seating accommodations.

SAMPLE OF WINES PRODUCED AT THIS AWARD-WINNING WINERY

Wine	Style	Grapes
Red		
Chambourcin	Dry	Chambourcin
River Bluff Red	Dry	Norton
Prairie Barn Red	Sweet	Frontenac
White		
Chardonel	Dry	Chardonel
Traminette	Dry	Traminette
Prairie Dew	Sweet	Chardonel
Vignoles	Sweet	Vignoles
Other		
Prairie Barn Blush	Blush	St. Croix

Other

Gift items and assortments of Illinois foods are available for take-out or consumption at the winery. They provide live music every week, as well as host dinner theaters. They offer rentals for weddings and private events. They also offer spiced wines, sangria, and other types of wine drinks.

Contact and Directions

23753 Lounsberry Road, Oakford, IL 62673. Events@HillPrairieWinery.com. (217) 635-9900. Thirty miles north of Springfield on Route 97, one-quarter mile south of Oakford.

Indian Creek Vineyard. *Author's collection.*

INDIAN CREEK VINEYARD

Owner
Fred Sams

History
The current owner purchased the winery in 1998. This winery takes its name from the creek bordering the vineyard, near land that once was home to Pottawatomie Indians. The farm has been in the family since 1836. The "Old Red Barn," once housing cows and hay, now constitutes the wine shop and tasting room. Fred was born and raised on this farm and is very proud of the winery's growth under his care.

SAMPLE OF GRAPES GROWN

Grape Name	Acreage
Frontenac	3
Maréchal Foch	3

Winery
Tasting room hours:
May–December,
Saturday–Sunday, 1 PM–5 PM.
Seating: 20.

Other
Items on sale include glasses and wine accessories.

Contact and Directions
9669 Vineyard Road, Toulon, IL 61483. (309) 286-5302. indiancreek@nbsmail
.net. One and a half miles north of Taudry, on Vineyard Road.

SAMPLE OF WINES PRODUCED OFF-SITE BY FOX VALLEY WINERY

Wine	Style	Grapes
Red		
Cabernet	Dry	Cabernet
Cabernet/Petite Sirah	Semidry	Cabernet, Petite Sirah
Concord	Sweet	Concord
White		
Traminette	Semidry	Traminettte
Niagara	Sweet	Niagara
Other		
Blush	Semisweet	Blend

KICKAPOO CREEK WINERY

Owner
Dr. David Conner

History
Kickapoo Creek Winery has been a large farm, a horse track, and most recently, a commercial nursery supplying garden centers and homeowners with premium plants, before being converted into a banquet center and winery. This family-owned winery began in 2001, when Dr. Conner began planting grapes, eventually covering fourteen acres. Kate Taylor is the winemaker. The Creek restaurant opened in July 2013.

SAMPLE OF GRAPES GROWN

Grape Name	Acreage
Cayuga White	0.5
Frontenac Gris	1
Marquette	2
Norton	1
NY 70	1
NY 73	1
NY 76	1
Prairie Star	2

Winery
Tasting room hours:
March–December,
Tuesday–Saturday, 11 AM–6 PM,
and Sunday, NOON–5 PM.
Winter, Saturday–Sunday,
NOON–5 PM.

Kickapoo Creek Winery's patio. *Courtesy of Kickapoo Creek Winery.*

SAMPLE OF WINES PRODUCED AT THIS AWARD-WINNING WINERY

Wine	Style	Grapes
Red		
Marquette	Dry	Marquette
Red October	Dry	Chancellor, Norton
Nookeenay	Sweet	Blend
White		
Misty Creek	Dry	Cayuga white
Pêche Blanc	Sweet	Seyval Blanc, peach flavor
Sun Kiss	Semisweet	Seyval Blanc, Vignoles

Other

Souvenirs are for sale in the winery. Lunch is served daily. The winery hosts events such as weddings and offers a winery tour. There is a walking trail that allows visitors to roam the grounds.

Contact and Directions

6605 N. Smith Road, Edwards, IL 61528. (309) 495-9463. kcw@kickapoocreek winery.com. Just east of Peoria, off I-74.

LAKE HILL WINERY AND BANQUET HALL

Owners
Craig Wear and Anita Wear; Maddie Gronewold, general manager

History
Lake Hill Winery was founded in 2010 by Craig Wear and Anita Wear. While on a rotation for pharmacy school in southeastern Australia in 2003, Craig first got the idea for a winery. He didn't even like wine at the time but was intrigued by the wine-making process and the beautiful vineyards. Once back in Hancock County, Craig began to explore the idea again. With the surrounding communities being supportive of their other businesses, Craig and Anita wanted to do something that would give back to the area, create jobs, and fill multiple voids. The idea for Lake Hill Winery was born.

In 2010 the Wears purchased approximately sixty-three acres of land west of Carthage Lake. Work began on the wine production building, which was completed in September 2010. The vineyard was next, with the first day of planting on April 1, 2011; the vineyard was completed in June 2011. The outdoor wedding gazebo and bridge were completed in the summer of 2011, with the first outdoor wedding held on October 1, 2011. Construction began on the banquet hall/tasting room in late May, 2011 and was mostly completed by New Year's Eve 2011, which was Lake Hill Winery's grand opening.

SAMPLE OF GRAPES GROWN

Grape Name	Acreage
Catawba	0.8
Concord	0.8
Frontenac	0.8
Frontenac Gris	0.8
Traminette	0.8

Winery
Tasting room hours:
April–Thanksgiving,
Wednesday–Thursday, 4 PM–9 PM;
Friday, 4 PM–MIDNIGHT;
Saturday, NOON–MIDNIGHT;
Sunday, NOON–6 PM.
Thanksgiving–March,
Friday, 4 PM–MIDNIGHT;
Saturday, NOON–MIDNIGHT;
Sunday, NOON–6 PM.
Seating: tasting room, 60; deck, 80; wedding ceremony area, over 400; banquet hall, over 400; smaller party room, 120.

Other
Items for sale: wine woozies, Horselick T-shirts, wine coasters, handbags, kitchen towels, wine napkins, magnets, and more. They have an Annual Backwoods Festival in the summer with food, boat races, and several bands. They also book wedding/ receptions, comedy shows, graduation parties, company dinners, and bands.

Wine bottles and the lake at Lake Hill Winery and Banquet Hall. *Courtesy of Lake Hill Winery and Banquet Hall.*

SAMPLE OF WINES PRODUCED

Wine	Style	Grapes
Red		
Norton	Dry	Norton
Blackhawk	Semisweet	Corot Noir, Concord, Niagara, Norton
Horselick	Sweet	Concord
White		
Chardonel	Dry	Chardonel, Seyval Blanc
Lincoln's Noose	Semidry	Traminette
1812	Semisweet	Vidal
Duck Hat	Sweet	Niagara
Other		
Chocolate Strawberry	Dessert red	Chancellor

Contact and Directions

1822 E. County Road 1540, Carthage, IL 62321. (217) 357-2675. info@lakehill winery.com. When heading west on IL 136 through Carthage, turn north at the Morton Building Production site. There is a "Tourist Attraction" sign as well. Continue around the curve, and follow the sign north to Lake Hill Winery. It is a half mile up the road on the right. There will be another sign to the parking lot.

MACKINAW VALLEY VINEYARD AND WINERY

Owners

Paul Hahn and Diane Hahn and family

History

Mackinaw Valley Vineyard and Winery is situated on ninety-six acres with fourteen acres used for grape vineyards; remaining acreage is for private use and corn and soybean production. Paul Hahn was working full-time as a building contractor and part-time as a farmer when he purchased the property in 1990 to build the family home and farm. He built a Victorian-style house and dug a 2.5-acre lake at the same time as digging the home foundation and began landscaping the areas adjacent to the home. He continued corn and soybean production on the farm acreage. In 1998 he saw an ad in an agricultural publication about growing wine grapes in Illinois. He attended a weekend seminar at Wollersheim Winery in Wisconsin and came home inspired and began planting grapes. Mackinaw Valley Vineyard often uses the tag line in advertising "Wine Country in your own Backyard" when talking about the look and feel of the vineyard and winery property.

SAMPLE OF GRAPES GROWN

Grape Name	Acreage
Baco Noir	1
Cayuga White	1
Corot Noir	1
Edelweiss	0.25
Frontenac	1
Maréchal Foch	1
Marquette	0.25
St. Croix	0.25
St. Pepin	0.25
Seyval Blanc	2
Table grapes	0.25
Vignoles	2

Winery

Tasting room hours (call for exact hours, as they may vary): May–November, Monday–Friday, 11 AM–6 PM; Saturday, 11 AM–11 PM; Sunday, NOON–5 PM. Seating: tasting room, 50; outdoor deck, 150; pavilion, 310.

Contact and Directions

33633 State Route 9, Mackinaw, IL 61755. (309) 359-9463. mackinawwinery03 @gmail.com. Midway between Peoria and Bloomington. Ten miles east of I-155 on State Route 9; exit in Tremont and go 16 miles west of the I-55 on State Route 9 exit in Bloomington.

Tasting room at Mackinaw Valley Vineyard and Winery. *Courtesy of Larry Lueallen.*

*T*he tasting room and wine-processing room were completed in 2003, the year the winery opened to the public. The home is situated on a glacial moraine with the tasting room built off the second story providing a unique thirty-mile view of the surrounding valley through its two-story viewing window. The winery currently hosts numerous weddings, receptions, events, concerts, and festivals. Paul has built an outdoor pavilion space with seating for up to three hundred people that is primarily used for festivals, receptions, and larger parties. There have been additional deck seating areas added to enjoy the views, as well as a small lake gazebo and a deck with pergola roof in the vineyard for hosting wedding ceremonies. These two areas are in addition to the large lake gazebo, where weddings and evening concerts are held. There have been two additional bar and three additional bathroom facilities added along with two bridal changing rooms.

SAMPLE OF WINES PRODUCED AT THIS AWARD-WINNING WINERY

Wine	Style	Grapes
Red		
Mackinaw Reserve	Dry	Baco Noir, Maréchal Foch
Alexander's Conquest	Off dry	Maréchal Foch, Frontenac, Cabernet Sauvignon
Carly's Creation	Sweet	Concord
White		
Priscilla's Passion	Dry	La Crosse
Seyval Blanc	Dry	Seyval Blanc
Vignoles	Dry	Vignoles
St. Pepin	Semidry	St. Pepin
Seyval Blanc	Sweet	Seyval Blanc
Vignoles	Sweet	Vignoles

Other

In 2013 they expanded the gift shop and tasting room areas. The vineyards host the International Music, Wine, and Beer Festival; the Art and Wine Festival; and the Harvest Festival. They also host concerts June through September and Murder Mystery Dinners and trivia nights in the winter and early spring. They have hosted a triathlon, a vineyard walk-run for charity, and a symphony orchestra concert and have even screened an original movie on a giant inflatable screen. The vineyard hosts popular educational tours and tastings for agriculture students and business groups. Items for sale: wine accessories, wine-themed T-shirts for men and women, gift shop items, art made by local artisans—a selection of blown-glass items, wood-crafted bottle holders and stoppers, pottery, confectionary artisan chocolates from the chocolatier in Bloomington, and artisan cheeses from Ropp Jersey Cheese in Normal.

Panorama at Mackinaw Valley Vineyard and Winery. *Courtesy of Larry Lueallen.*

Ridge View Winery's vineyards. *Courtesy of Ridge View Winery, LLC.*

RIDGE VIEW WINERY, LLC

Owners
Larry Hanold and Phyllis Hanold

History
This winery's terrain has variations from 230 feet from the ridge tops to the creeks below. The winery is located on a ridge two hundred feet above the McKee Creek valley. Both the upper and lower decks provide a panoramic view of the surrounding wooded ridges. The owners planted twenty-two hundred Chardonel grapes on four acres in 2000. In 2002 another 1.3 acres of Frontenac, Maréchal Foch, Corot Noir, and GR 7 were added to make a total of three thousand vines. Construction on the 10,600-square-foot winery was begun in September 2005 and opened June 1, 2007.

SAMPLE OF GRAPES GROWN

Grape Name	Acreage
Chardonel	4
Corot Noir	0.1
Frontenac	1
GR 7	0.1
Maréchal Foch	0.1

Winery
Tasting room hours:
April–November,
Tuesday–Thursday, 11 AM–6 PM;
Friday, 11 AM–10 PM;
Saturday, 11 AM–10 PM;
Sunday, NOON–6 PM.
December 1–March 30,
Thursday, 11 AM–6 PM;
Friday–Saturday, 11 AM–10 PM;
Sunday, NOON–6 PM. Seating:
tasting room, 90; banquet hall, 160.

SAMPLE OF WINES PRODUCED

Wine	Style	Grapes
Red		
Corot Noir	Dry	Corot Noir
Norton	Dry	Norton
Signature Red	Dry	Noiret, Corot Noir, Maréchal Foch
Frontenac	Semidry	Frontenac
McKee Creek Red	Semisweet	Frontenac, Corot Noir
White		
Chardonel	Dry	Chardonel
Traminette	Semidry	Traminette
Summer Chardonel	Semisweet	Chardonel
Vignoles	Semisweet	Vignoles
Edelweiss	Sweet	Edelweiss

Other
The winery hosts numerous festivals and musical events throughout the year.

Contact and Directions
529 200N Avenue, Mt. Sterling, IL 62353. (217) 289-3300. request@ridgeview winery.com. The winery is 9½ miles southwest of Mt. Sterling.

SLEEPY CREEK VINEYARDS

Owners
Joe Taylor and Dawn Taylor

History
The vineyard was started in 2002, and the winery opened in 2007. They make all their wines on the premises and grow ten acres of grapes. They currently produce thirty thousand bottles of wine a year and often cannot keep up with demand. The winery hosts annual events and festivals. Above the working winery they have opened a rustic retreat they call the "bed and wine."

Tony Jacobson and Kayla Johnson of Sleepy Creek Vineyards. *Courtesy of Midwest Wine Press.*

Other

The winery has both a gift shop and an art gallery. They also have entertainment as well as a "B&W" (bed-and-wine) vacation rental. It's like a bed-and-breakfast, but they give a bottle of wine instead of breakfast.

Contact and Directions

8254 E. 1425 North Road, Fairmount, IL 61841. (217) 733-0330. info @sleepycreekvineyards.com. Twenty-five miles from Champaign and a few minutes from Danville; take exit 206 off I-74 and go south 3½ miles.

SAMPLE OF GRAPES GROWN

Grape Name	Acreage
Frontenac	4
La Crescent	4
Léon Millot	0.5
Maréchal Foch	0.25
Rougeon	0.25
Vignoles	1

Winery

Tasting room hours:
Monday–Thursday, 10 AM–6 PM;
Friday–Saturday, 10 AM–8 PM;
Sunday, NOON–6 PM.
Seating: 75.

SAMPLE OF WINES PRODUCED

Wine	Style	Grapes
Red		
Bull Headed	Dry	Chambourcin, Rougeon
Norton and Noiret	Dry	Norton, Noiret
Little Woody	Semidry	Léon Millot, Maréchal Foch
Hen Pecked	Semisweet	Frontenac
White		
Dreamer	Semidry	Cayuga, Vidal Blanc
Sour Puss	Semisweet	La Crescent, Vignoles, Traminette
Scapegoat	Sweet	Cayuga, La Crosse, Niagara
Other		
Bashful Ewe	Blush	Frontenac

SPIRIT KNOB WINERY

Owner
Matt Schulte

History
Matt started making wine in the mid-1990s, inspired by his father. He planted grapes in 1999 and received a license in 2002. The winery operated out of the family basement for six years until they were able to build the existing winery in 2007, with a beautiful view of the Mississippi River valley. Cedar trees were cut down to make way for the building, but the wood was used for interior furniture, the bar, the mantle, and trusses. According to Matt, don't miss the hospitality, the view, and the fun of this winery experience.

Spirit Knob Winery's fireplace. *Courtesy of Spirit Knob Winery.*

SAMPLE OF GRAPES GROWN

Grape Name	Acreage
Chambourcin	1.5
Chardonel	1
Norton	0.5

Winery
Tasting room hours:
April–December, Wednesday, Thursday, Saturday, and Sunday, 1 PM–5 PM; Friday, 1 PM–6 PM.
January–March,
Friday, 1 PM–6 PM;
Saturday–Sunday, 1 PM–5 PM.
Seating: 150.

SAMPLE OF WINES PRODUCED AT THIS AWARD-WINNING WINERY

Wine	Style	Grapes
Red		
Chambourcin	Dry	Chambourcin
Norton	Dry	Norton
White		
Chardonel	Dry	Chardonel
Traminette	Semisweet	Traminette
Vignoles	Sweet	Vignoles

Other

The winery hosts weddings and other events.

Contact and Directions

2211 E. 640th Place, Ursa, IL 62376. (217) 964-2678. spiritknob@adams.net.
US 24 to IL 96 to County Road 640.

THE VILLAGE VINEYARD AND WINERY

Owners

Gordon and Brenda Cantrell

History

The Cantrell family planted three acres of grapes in 2001. They had, however, been introduced to wine making already in 1997. They first sold grapes to other wineries but now produce their own bottles. Before their wine making, they were corn and soybean farmers.

Sample of Grapes Grown

Some of the grapes grown are Edelweiss, Frontenac, GR 7, Norton, Traminette, and Vignoles.

Gordon Cantrell of the Village Vineyard and Winery. *Author's collection.*

Winery
Tasting room hours: Friday, 5 PM–10 PM; Saturday, NOON–11 PM; Sunday, NOON–6 PM.

SAMPLE OF WINES PRODUCED

Wine	Style	Grapes
Red		
Corot Noir	Dry	Corot Noir
Norton	Dry	Norton
White		
Vignoles	Semidry	Vignoles
Traminette	Semisweet	Traminette

Other
The winery hosts a "Hallow-wine" party, has live music, and has hosted the Golden Retriever Rescue fund-raiser.

Contact and Directions
337 N. Vermont, Camp Point, IL 62320. (217) 509-9463. vvandw@adams.net. Two blocks east of Bailey Park in Camp Point.

THE WALNUT STREET WINERY

Owner
Loren Shanle

History
The winery makes small-batch wines using grapes from many different areas. They have a bocce ball court that allows visitors to relax and enjoy a game while they sip wines. They are near the Lincoln Presidential Museum and invite everyone coming to see that impressive collection to visit the winery as well (and of course, Illinois state legislators may stop by when the legislature is in session).

Sample of Grapes Grown
The winery does not grow its own grapes.

Winery
Tasting room hours: Monday, 2 PM–8 PM; Tuesday, 2 PM–11 PM; Wednesday–Saturday, NOON–11 PM; Sunday, 1 PM–8 PM.

SAMPLE OF WINES PRODUCED

Wine	Style	Grapes
Red		
Shiraz	Dry	Shiraz
Zinfandel	Dry	Zinfandel
White		
Chardonnay	Dry	Chardonnay

Other
The winery has a garden and hosts weddings, class reunions, office parties, and other events. The bocce ball court is sixty feet long and thirteen feet wide.

Contact and Directions
309 S. Walnut Street, Rochester, IL 62563. (217) 498-9800. Off Route 29, 7 miles east of the state capitol in Springfield.

The Walnut Street Winery's wine garden. *Courtesy of the Walnut Street Winery.*

Vintners Steve Deiro (*background*) and Phil Lofy (*foreground*) bottling wine at the Walnut Street Winery. *Courtesy of the Walnut Street Winery.*

WHITE OAK VINEYARDS

Owners
Rudolf Hofmann and Mary Hofmann

History
The vineyard was established in 2003 with 2.5 acres. Every year they have added vines, and now are up to 10.5 acres or approximately five thousand plants. In 2010 they purchased the neighboring property (117 acres) and converted the log cabin home into the winery operation and tasting room. The tasting room opened in May 2011. At the IGGVA event in 2013, five of their wines were selected to represent Illinois at the ITB Convention in Berlin—the world's largest travel fair. Inspiration for becoming winemakers began during their years in Ebrach, Germany.

SAMPLE OF GRAPES GROWN

Grape Name	Acreage
Cayuga White	1
Frontenac	2
Maréchal Foch	1
St. Croix	1
Seyval Blanc	1
Steuben	2
Traminette	1.5

Winery
Tasting room hours:
March–October,
Monday–Thursday, 10 AM–6 PM;
Friday–Saturday, 10 AM–8 PM;
Sunday, 1 PM–5 PM.
Winter hours (November, December, February),
Monday, 10 AM–6 PM; Thursday, 10 AM–6 PM; Friday–Saturday, 10 AM–8 PM; Sunday, 1 PM–5 PM.

Mary Hofmann of White Oak Vineyards. *Courtesy of Midwest Wine Press.*

SAMPLE OF WINES PRODUCED AT THIS AWARD-WINNING WINERY

Wine	Style	Grapes
Red		
Bernese Red	Dry	Frontenac
Landhaus	Dry	Norton
Windmill Dreams	Semisweet	Steuben
Wintertraum	Semisweet	Chambourcin
White		
WeisseEiche	Dry	Cayuga White
Golden Days	Semisweet	Seyval Blanc
Heimat	Semisweet	Riesling
Sonnenschein	Semisweet	Vignoles

Other

Caps, T-shirts, napkins, local cheeses, beer, and other beverages are available for sale in the winery. The facility has room available for birthdays, weddings, and music events.

Contact and Directions

8621 East 2100 North Road, Carlock, IL 61725. (309) 376-3027. hofmannmary @msn.com. Near Bloomington, off I-74.

WILLETT'S WINERY AND CELLAR

Owners
Cris Willett

History
Dan Willett and Cris Willett began this winery. Dan passed away in 2011, but Cris continues to build its reputation. This winery has three locations: two in Manito (one being a restaurant), and one in Peoria. It all started in 2005, five years after the planting of a five-acre vineyard near Spring Lake. The building dates from 1893 and was rebuilt after a fire in 1914. The original building housed a harness shop. In 2010 Willett's Winery expanded to include a production room and the Ironstone Room Restaurant. The banquet room, completed in 2011, holds up to 180 guests.

Sample of Grapes Grown
Grapes include Concord, Frontenac, La Crosse, Léon Millot, Noiret, Seyval Blanc, and Vignoles, grown on six or seven acres total.

Winery
Tasting room hours: Monday–Saturday, NOON–5 PM. There are two locations (see below).

Brad Beam pushing skids at Willett's Winery and Cellar. *Courtesy of Midwest Wine Press.*

Wine	Style	Grapes
Red		
St. Croix	Semidry	St. Croix
Hometown Red	Sweet	Concord, Villard
White		
Seyval Blanc	Dry	Seyval Blanc
Vignoles	Semisweet	Vignoles

Other

The winery hosts live music and mystery theaters, among other events.

Contact and Directions

5201 W. War Memorial Drive, suite 322, Peoria, IL 61615; 105 E. Market Street, Manito, IL 61546. (309) 968-7070. willetswinery@yahoo.com. There is a new location: Willett's Wines at Grand Prairie.

WYLDEWOOD CELLARS WINERY

Owner

Dr. John A. Brewer, president

History

The company began in 1995, and the Illinois location opened in 2010. The family hails in part from the Champaign area and wanted to move back home. St. Joseph, Illinois, welcomed them, and they began a family business. They began wine making to produce good quality wine at good prices. At the main winery in Kansas there are about five acres of elderberries, grapes, and other fruit. Currently the Illinois location does bottle and ferment some of the wines in St. Joseph, but eventually they plan to find some land nearby and build a bigger facility for more manufacturing and even a banquet room.

Sample of Grapes Grown

The Illinois winery does not currently grow grapes.

Winery

Tasting room hours: St. Joseph location, Monday–Saturday, 10 AM–6 PM; Sundays, NOON–5 PM.

Sample of Wines Produced

Various types of grape and fruit wines, including their award-winning Kansas Vineyard Wines, are produced.

Wyldewood Cellars Winery's front door. *Courtesy of Wyldewood Cellars Winery.*

Contact and Directions

218 E. Lincoln Street, St. Joseph, IL 61873. (217) 469-9463 tracietrotter@att.net. Take I-74 going east to exit 192, take a right and continue straight into town until you reach the corner of Lincoln and Main.

SOUTH CENTRAL
Region

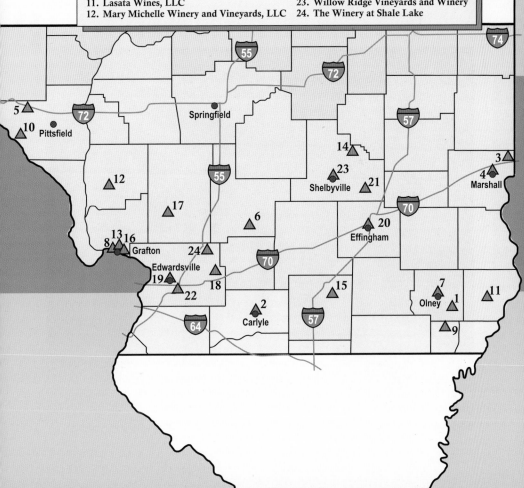

South Central Region Wineries

1. Berryville Vineyards
2. Bretz Wildlife Lodge and Winery
3. Cameo Vineyards
4. Castle Finn Vineyard and Winery, Inc.
5. Collver Family Winery
6. Forsee Vineyards and Winery
7. Fox Creek Vineyards, Inc.
8. Grafton Winery and Brewhaus
9. Homestead Vineyards
10. Hopewell Winery
11. Lasata Wines, LLC
12. Mary Michelle Winery and Vineyards, LLC
13. Mary Michelle Winery Tasting Room
14. Niemerg Family Winery
15. Orchard View Winery
16. PiasaWinery and Pub
17. Plainview Vineyard
18. Roundhouse Wine Company
19. Springers Creek Winery
20. Tuscan Hills Winery
21. Vahling Vineyards and Winery
22. Villa Marie Winery
23. Willow Ridge Vineyards and Winery
24. The Winery at Shale Lake

BERRYVILLE VINEYARDS

Owner
Eric Pool

History
All wines at this South Central Illinois location are 100 percent estate grown and bottled in this winery. Eric, who grew up in the area, is proud of the winery's many sustainable farming methods. For example, they do not till, as this would contribute to erosion and the release of CO_2. They use only organic fertilizer, and no pre-emergent herbicides. The winery also uses sustainable practices: they use no plastic, use only geothermal heating and cooling, and have a wood stove for heat.

Sample of Grapes Grown
Grapes include Chambourcin, Cynthiana, Seyval Blanc, and Vignoles.

Winery
Tasting room hours: March–December, Saturday, NOON–5 PM.

Other
This winery appears in many local festivals and events.

Berryville Vineyards' tasting room exterior. *Courtesy of Berryville Vineyards.*

Wine	Style	Grapes
Red		
Cynthiana	Dry	Cynthiana
Proprietor's Red	Dry	Chambourcin
White		
Dragonfly	Dry	Seyval Blanc
Traminette	Dry	Traminette
White Squirrel	Semi sweet	Vignoles

Contact and Directions

1910 N. Prairie Road, Claremont, IL 62421. (618) 456-2335. clusterbuster75 @yahoo.com. They are 3 miles north of Berryville or 1 mile west and 6 miles south of the Lawrence County prison.

BRETZ WILDLIFE LODGE AND WINERY

Owners

Sandy and Matt Bretz

History

The two owners loved South Africa, and their travels inspired the lodge, as well as the "lodge" concept. They opened their doors in 2008. The lodge features a rustic and traditional décor with many mementos of their travels through Africa and elsewhere.

Sample of Grapes Grown

This winery does not grow its own grapes but produces its own fruit wines.

Winery

Tasting room hours: Monday, 3 PM–9 PM; Tuesday–Wednesday, 7 AM–9 PM; Thursday, 7 AM–11 PM; Friday–Saturday, 7 AM–2 AM; Sunday, 9 AM–9 PM.

Other

This winery has a lodge and restaurant.

Contact and Directions

15469 State Route 127, Carlyle, IL 62231. (618) 594-8830. info@wildlifelodge andwinery.com.

Bretz Wildlife Lodge and Winery's sign. *Courtesy of Bretz Wildlife Lodge and Winery.*

SAMPLE OF WINES PRODUCED

Wine	Style	Grapes
Red		
Safari Red	Dry	Chambourcin
Kudu Red	Semisweet	Chambourcin
Passion Cheetah	Sweet	Concord
White		
Serengeti White	Dry	Chardonel
Shu-Lula	Semidry	Vidal Blanc
Lion's Eyes Riesling	Semisweet	Riesling
Mystic White	Semisweet	Niagara, Riesling
Serenity	Sweet	Villard Blanc

Cஜ

CAMEO VINEYARDS

Owners
Dan Webb and Sonya Webb

History
Perched on bluffs overlooking panoramic views of the hillside vineyards and the Embarras River valley, the winery was built using the family's grandfather's barn (circa 1900). It all started in 1991 when the owners planted seventy grapevines. The winery opened in 2002. They grow several varieties of grapes, which they craft into wine.

SAMPLE OF GRAPES GROWN

Grape Name	Acreage
Cayuga White	1
Chambourcin	1
Norton	1
Vidal Blanc	1
Vignoles	1
Villard Blanc	1

Winery

Tasting room hours:
Tuesday–Saturday, 10 AM–5 PM;
Sunday, NOON–5 PM.

Contact and Directions

400 Mill Road, Greenup, IL 62428.
(217) 923-9963.
cameo@cameowine.com.

SAMPLE OF WINES PRODUCED AT THIS AWARD-WINNING WINERY

Wine	Style	Grapes
Red		
Chambourcin	Dry	Chambourcin
Norton	Dry	Norton
Country Concord	Sweet	Concord
White		
Pink Catawba	Semisweet	Catawba
Vidal Blanc	Semisweet	Vidal Blanc
Powder Hill White	Sweet	Vignoles

Cameo Vineyards and grapes. *Courtesy of Megan Presnall/IGGVA.*

CASTLE FINN VINEYARD AND WINERY, INC.

Owners
Rob Morgan, Bart Morgan, and Sonya Stephens

History
Castle Finn opened in 2010 with a banquet room that hosts weddings, parties, showers, and more. The owners come from a farming background (corn, soybeans, and alfalfa) and wanted to diversify. They had been making wine as a hobby for years but didn't know at the time they would go commercial.

SAMPLE OF GRAPES GROWN

Grape Name	Acreage
Cayuga White	0.5
Chambourcin	0.5
Fredonia	0.5
Frontenac	0.5
Niagara	0.5

Winery
Tasting room hours:
Tuesday–Thursday, 10 AM–6 PM;
Friday, 10 AM–8 PM;
Saturday, 10 AM–6 PM;
Sunday, NOON–5 PM.
The tasting room remains open even during events.

SAMPLE OF WINES PRODUCED

Wine	Style	Grapes
Red		
Bell Ridge Red	Dry	Chambourcin
Red Brick Red	Semisweet	Blend
Castle Finn Red	Sweet	Blend
White		
Bell Ridge White	Dry	Blend
Castle Finn White	Semisweet	Cayuga White
Moonlight Minuet	Sweet	Niagara

Other
The winery hosts events such as a Christmas party, murder mystery, comedy night, and others.

Contact and Directions
1288 N. 1200th Street, Marshall, IL 62441. (217) 463-2600. Contact Sonya at sstephens@castlefinnwinery.com. From I-70 go north on Route 1 for 5.5 miles; then turn left on Bell Ridge Road. Follow the road to 225N until arriving at 1200E and turn south. The winery is approximately 1 mile from there.

Castle Finn Vineyard and Winery, Inc. *Courtesy of Castle Finn Vineyard and Winery, Inc.*

COLLVER FAMILY WINERY

Owner
James Collver and Tim Collver

History
The winery opened in 2002 and is still family owned. They are proud to have been the first winery to open in west central Illinois in over one hundred years. All wines are produced and bottled at the winery from French American hybrid grapes.

SAMPLE OF GRAPES GROWN

Grape Name	Acreage
Cayuga White	1
Chambourcin	1
Chardonel	0.5
Traminette	3
Vidal Blanc	1
Vignoles	3

Winery
Tasting room hours:
Wednesday–Saturday, 10 AM–5 PM; Sunday, NOON–5 PM.
Seating: 16; back room/production room, 120.

Collver Family Winery. *Author's collection.*

SAMPLE OF WINES PRODUCED AT THIS AWARD-WINNING WINERY

Wine	Style	Grapes
Red		
Red Rooster	Semisweet	Maréchal Foch
White		
Yorkshire White	Dry	Blend
Vidal Blanc	Semidry	Vidal Blanc
White Hen	Semisweet	Blend
Octoberfest	Sweet	Chardonel, Vignoles

Other
Miscellaneous wine accessories are available in the gift shop.

Contact and Directions
2 Rooster Way, Barry, IL 62312. (217) 335-3279. timcollver@collverfamilywinery
.com. Take I-72 exit 20 or Highway 106. Barry is on Hill behind Jiffy Stop.

FORSEE VINEYARDS AND WINERY

Owner
Diane Forsee

History
Nestled among a landscape of rolling hills, this winery began as a cattle farm. They sold cuts of beef from their beef herd. Customers came for an opportunity to see the cows, watch hay baling, and other activities but hesitated to leave. The family had no preparations for them and pondered adding facilities but asked, "What goes with steak?" The answer was easy. They began visiting wineries in Missouri and Illinois to ask questions, took a wine-making course, and joined seminars on growing grapes. They planted in 2003 and raised the winery in 2006, opening the tasting room in February 2008. The family has a passion for growing grapes and letting them interpret the environment. Their motto: Love what you do!

SAMPLE OF GRAPES GROWN

Grape Name	Acreage
Chardonel	1
Corot Noir	1
Niagara	1
Norton	1
NY 76	1
Traminette	2
Vignoles	1

Winery
Tasting room hours:
open year-round,
Thursday by appointment,
Friday–Saturday, NOON–10 PM,
Sunday, NOON–6 PM.
Seating: inside, 45; pavilion, 90;
patios, 45.

Other
They carry three flavors of sangria made fresh with Forsee Cherry wine, bottled beer, and limited gift shop items. Summer sausage, assorted cheese, and crackers are available; however, they encourage visitors to bring a picnic basket. They have accommodations for private parties, rehearsal dinners, and vineyard weddings. Facilities are accessible to people with disabilities.

Contact and Directions
18165 N. Fourth Avenue, Coffeen, IL 62017. (217) 534-6347. winemaster@forsee vineyards.com. From I-55 south, exit 52 at Litchfield. Follow Route 127 through Litchfield and Hillsboro. At Route 185 turn left and drive 9 miles. Turn right onto East 19th Road and turn right on North 4th Road.

Forsee Vineyards and Winery. *Courtesy of Forsee Vineyards and Winery.*

SAMPLE OF WINES PRODUCED

Wine	Style	Grapes
Red		
Corot Noir	Dry	Corot Noir
Norton	Dry	Norton
Okaw Red	Off dry	Corot Noir, Léon Millot
Endless Summer	Sweet	Norton
White		
Chardonel	Dry	Chardonel
Okaw White	Semisweet	Chardonel, Vignoles
Traminette	Semisweet	Traminette
Niagara	Sweet	Niagara
Vignoles	Sweet	Vignoles
Other		
Starboard	Dessert	Corot Noir
Starboard	Dessert	Norton
Montgomery Co. Sparkling	Semisweet	Chardonel, Vignoles

FOX CREEK VINEYARDS, INC.

Owner
Gordon Schnepper

History
The vineyard and winery were a continuous stop in the evolution of southeastern Illinois farming for this fourth-generation family of Illinois farmers. F. Schnepper's ownership of the farm evolved from general farming to dairy, then to swine, and finally to grapes. They incorporated in 1999. With eight varieties of grapes planted on three acres, they are currently producing fifteen wines from grapes with five other fruit and berry wines, all grown in the immediate area.

Sample of Grapes Grown
Grapes include Cayuga White, Chambourcin, Frontier, Frontier Gris, Maréchal Foch, Seyval Blanc, Ventura, and Vidal Blanc.

Winery
Tasting room hours: Friday–Saturday, 10 AM–6 PM; Sunday, 1 PM–6 PM; also by appointment. Seating: 40–50.

Fox Creek Vineyards, Inc., wines featured at Oak Park's Uncork Illinois. *Courtesy of Elliot Weisenberg.*

Wine	Style	Grapes
Red		
Deer Farm Red	Dry	Chambourcin
Hearthside I Red	Semidry	Blend
Deep Purple	Sweet	Chambourcin
Hearthside II Red	Sweet	Blend
White		
Cayuga White	Off dry	Cayuga white
Deep Farm White	Sweet	Blend
Blush		
Vixen Cheek	Semisweet	Catawba

Other
Wine accessories are for sale in the winery.

Contact and Directions
5502 N. Fox Road, Olney, IL 62450. (618) 392-0418. wines@foxcreekwinery.com. Take Route 130 north from Olney to Deer Farm Lane/County Road 1400N; turn left and go west 1 mile to Fox Road/County Road 1000E, then left (south) ¼ mile to driveway; follow the drive.

GRAFTON WINERY AND BREWHAUS

Owners
Mike and Lori Nikonovich

History
Opened in December 2008, the winery is situated in the heart of historic Grafton along the Great Rivers Scenic Byway. The winery overlooks the confluence of the Mississippi and Illinois Rivers. From the terrace, you can see eagles soaring in the winter, the wildlife and surrounding vegetation coming to life in the spring, beautiful sunsets and pleasure boats on the river in the summer, and of course changing leaf colors in the fall.

Sample of Grapes Grown
The winery does not grow its own grapes.

Winery
Tasting room hours: Monday–Thursday, 11 AM–7 PM; Friday–Saturday, 11 AM–9 PM; Sunday, NOON–7 PM.

Grafton Winery and Brewhaus. *Courtesy of Grafton Winery and Brewhaus.*

SAMPLE OF WINES PRODUCED AT THIS AWARD-WINNING WINERY

Wine	Style	Grapes
Red		
Harbor Red	Dry	Cabernet Sauvignon, Zinfandel, Syrah
Captain's Blush	Semidry	Catawba
White		
Pinot Gris	Dry	Pinot Gris
Harbor White	Semidry	Vidal Blanc, Seyval Blanc, Vignoles, Cayuga, Muscat
Riverbend White	Sweet	Niagara

Other

Grafton Winery and Brewhaus also offers a quality experience in beers, along with their wine tasting. Mike Nikonovich Jr. has created a diverse and satisfying menu of beers. The Brewhaus and brewing facility is open Friday–Sunday and hosts parties and corporate events.

Contact and Directions

300 West Main Street, Grafton, IL 62037. (618) 786-3001. info@graftonwinery .com. Just forty-five minutes from downtown St. Louis, Missouri, and twenty minutes from St. Charles, Missouri.

HOMESTEAD VINEYARDS

Owner
Larry Hortin

History
This winery opened in 2012 as a brand-new location with no previous owners. This is the only winery in Edwards County. The family purchased the current homestead in 1975, on three-quarters of an acre with a two-bedroom home. Many years of improvements later, the fruits of their labor are evident. This family venture consists of Larry, his wife, Shirley, son Jason, brother-in-law Jerry, daughter-in-law Dawn, and grandsons Cooper and Curtis. They were able to open operations thanks to the voters of Edwards County Road District 1 who voted the district "wet."

Sample of Grapes Grown
Grapes include Cayuga White, Chambourcin, Concord, and Maréchal Foch.

Winery
Tasting room hours: Saturday–Sunday, NOON–5PM. Seating accommodations indoors with pleasant atmosphere outdoors.

Shirley working at Homestead Vineyards. *Courtesy of Homestead Vineyards.*

Homestead Vineyards wines. *Courtesy of Homestead Vineyards.*

SAMPLE OF WINES PRODUCED

Wine	Style	Grapes
Red		
Chambourcin	Dry	Chambourcin
Maréchal Foch	Dry	Maréchal Foch
Winter Solstice	Dry	Chambourcin, Maréchal Foch
White		
Cayuga White	Dry	Cayuga White
Summer Solstice	Sweet	Cayuga White

Other

Wines, wine racks, openers, candles, and more are available at the winery. They are a brand-new winery, and they will host weddings, parties, class reunions, and family reunions—just enjoy the grounds!

Contact and Directions

1785 County Road 775 E, West Salem, IL 62476. homesteadvineyards@hotmail .com. In West Salem go south on Broadway Street; the winery is ¾ mile on the right.

Hopewell Winery. *Author's Collection.*

HOPEWELL WINERY

History
This winery opened in 2007 on an acre of land, and they have now opened a winery with a banquet hall.

Sample of Grapes Grown
The winery does not grow its own grapes.

Winery
Tasting room hours: Friday–Saturday, 10 AM–6 PM; Sunday, NOON–5 PM.

SAMPLE OF WINES PRODUCED

Wine	Style	Grapes
Red		
Chambourcin	Dry	Chambourcin
Norton	Dry	Norton
White		
Chardonel	Dry	Chardonel
Vignoles	Dry	Vignoles
Hunter White	Semisweet	Blend
Other		
Quail Blush	Sweet	Blend

Other

The winery hosts events, and there is no rental fee. They can provide catering. They are known for their "shrimp and crawfish fest."

Contact and Directions

19048 US Highway 54, Rockport, IL 62370. (217) 285-2759. support@hopewell winery.com. Ten miles from I-72 and 5 miles from the Mississippi River, on Highway 54; 7 miles from Pittsfield, Illinois, and Louisiana, Missouri.

LASATA WINES, LLC

Owner

Brett Robling

History

Lasata is an Indian word meaning "place of peace." The winery was built in 2003 and opened in 2004, on land that was in the family for several generations. The site of the winery was formerly a home for hired workers. It was removed, and the new beautiful wooden building was built in 2003.

Other

The gift shop sells cheese, crackers, and other items. They also make customized gift baskets.

Lasata Wines, LLC. *Courtesy of Megan Presnall/IGGVA.*

SAMPLE OF GRAPES GROWN

Grape Name	Acreage
Cabernet Franc	0.33
Chambourcin	2
Cynthiana	0.4
DeChaunac	0.33
Seyval Blanc	0.5
Traminette	2.8
Vidal Blanc	1.5

Winery

Tasting room hours:
April–December,
Tuesday–Sunday, NOON–5 PM;
January–March, NOON–5 PM;
also by appointment.
Seating: approximately 40.

SAMPLE OF WINES PRODUCED

Wine	Style	Grapes
Red		
Chambourcin	Dry	Chambourcin
Cynthiana	Semidry	Cynthiana
Purple Passion	Sweet	Concord
Sweet Red	Sweet	Chambourcin
White		
Vintner's Select	Dry	Vidal Blanc
Dark Hollow	Sweet	Vidal Blanc
Illinois Sunset	Sweet	Seyval Blanc

Contact and Directions

Rural Route 2, Box 64B (Highway 33) Lawrenceville, IL 62439. (618) 884-1200.
Brett@lasatawines.com. One mile north of Westport on Highway 33, approximately 3 miles east of Highway 50.

MARY MICHELLE WINERY
AND VINEYARDS, LLC

Owner

Andy Litwack, winemaker

History

The winery began in 1999 when a group from Santa Barbara, California, wanted to explore wine making in the five counties surrounding the lower Illinois River where there had once been prominent grape production. They began planting grapes. The competition from California after World War II had made it difficult

Mary Michelle Winery and Vineyards, LLC. *Courtesy of Megan Presnall/IGGVA.*

for growers in the area to continue to make wine. The goal was affordable, world-class wines from Illinois. Andy Litwach, a Midwest native, has over thirty years' experience in the California wine industry. He utilized his University of California, Davis, graduate education to make wines in both the United States and Israel.

Sample of Grapes Grown
Grapes include Norton, Vidal Blanc, and others experimentally.

SAMPLE OF WINES PRODUCED AT THIS AWARD-WINNING WINERY

Wine	Style	Grapes
Red		
Norton	Dry	Norton
Velvet Red	Dry	Blend
White		
Chardonel	Dry	Chardonel
Velvet White	Sweet	Niagara
Other		
Ice Wine	Sweet	Vidal Blanc

Contact and Directions
Rural Route 2, Box 7A, Carrollton, IL 62016. (217) 942-6250. email@mary michellewinery.com

Niemerg Family Winery's tasting room. *Courtesy of Niemerg Family Winery.*

NIEMERG FAMILY WINERY

Owners
The Niemerg family

History
The winery opened in 2007, and the father-and-son trio of Don, Bill, and Dan produce a wide variety of wines. They conditioned the hundred-year-old building and continue to renovate the tasting room.

Sample of Grapes Grown
The winery does not produce its own grapes.

Winery
Tasting room hours: winter hours, Friday, 3 PM–8 PM; Saturday, 11 AM–8 PM; Sunday, NOON–5 PM; summer hours, Tuesday–Friday, NOON–8 PM; Saturday, 11 AM–8 PM; Sunday, NOON–5 PM.

Sample of Wines Produced
Various types of wines produced with grapes from Illinois, as well as other parts of the country.

Contact and Directions
301 S. Main Street, Findlay, IL 62534. (217) 756-5521. On Main Street in downtown Findlay, Illinois.

ORCHARD VIEW WINERY

Owner

Brad Mazanek

History

The winery was started in October 2007. Brad Mazanek had a dream: to take a barn in his backyard that housed livestock and turn it into a winery. It seemed impossible and sounded like a lot of hard work, but Brad is no stranger to hard work. The Mazaneks are well known in the little community of Alma. Their family name is synonymous in the area with fresh fruits such as apples, peaches, and nectarines. Brad knew he had the best apples and peaches, along with the desire to make a good wine. He then realized, "Why not grow grapes too?" He began a journey to slowly turn the cattle barn into a beautiful winery. He poured concrete in the old barn, installed heat in the floors, and put in a ceiling with beams—and of course air-conditioning. Another beautiful feature of the barn is upstairs, the hay loft turned into a banquet hall, where several couples have been married. In the back of the winery he put a production room to start the wine-making process. Just outside is a covered porch area where guests can watch the sunset while almost watching the grape vines grow. A fire pit is also available on chilly days.

SAMPLE OF GRAPES GROWN

Grape Name	Acreage
Noiret	1

Winery

Tasting room hours:
April–December,
Saturday–Sunday, 1 PM–6 PM.
Seating: 50.

Orchard View Winery. *Courtesy of Orchard View Winery.*

$\mathcal{B}$rad admits that wine making and owning a winery is a tricky business of balancing his love of farming and running a huge peach and apple orchard. His wife, Lisa, takes an important role in the business in the summer, greeting clients and doing wine tastings. She is employed as a full-time teacher in Kinmundy. They add to their current hours as time permits and enjoy the wine-making process as they continue to grow.

SAMPLE OF WINES PRODUCED

Wine	Style	Grapes
Red		
Noiret	Dry	Noiret
Norton	Dry	Norton

Other
The winery provides an excellent place to relax and enjoy wine.

Contact and Directions
307 Second Street, Alma, IL 62807. (618) 547-9911. lisamazanek@yahoo.com. They are 2 blocks west of Route 37 on Second Street, Alma.

PIASA WINERY AND PUB

Owner
Judy Wiemann (also owner of Villa Marie)

History
Father Marquette and Joliet recorded the legend of the Piasa bird as told by the Native Americans they met. The word means "bird that devours men." The winery named after this fearsome creature overlooks the confluence of the Mississippi and the Illinois Rivers. Judy Wiemann bought this property in 2007, although it had started in 1992 as the twelfth winery in Illinois.

Sample of Grapes Grown
Piasa does not grow its own grapes.

Winery
Tasting room hours: Monday–Thursday, 11 AM–9 PM; Friday–Saturday, 11 AM–?; Sunday, NOON–9 PM.

Piasa Winery and Pub. *Author's collection.*

Other

The winery hosts live music events.

Contact and Directions

225 West Main Street, Grafton, IL 62037. (618) 786-9463. piasawinery@hotmail
.com. The winery is north of St. Louis.

SAMPLE OF WINES PRODUCED

Wine	Style	Grapes
Red		
Chambourcin	Dry	Chambourcin
Norton	Dry	Norton
White		
Chautauqua Chardonel	Dry	Chardonel
Illini White	Sweet	Chardonel
Ouatoga Gold	Sweet	Muscat

PLAINVIEW VINEYARD

Owners

Albert Becker, Jackie Becker, and Shelby Becker

History

The winery was opened in 2007 although the owners planted a commercial vineyard from 1998 to 2002. Theirs was the first winery in Macoupin County. Plainview currently has twenty-two wines produced from seventeen grape varieties, the only grapes used to produce their wines. The location offers a shaded porch and lakeside picnicking facilities.

SAMPLE OF GRAPES GROWN

Grape Name	Acreage
Chambourcin	0.5
Concord	0.25
Léon Millot	0.5
Maréchal Foch	0.5
Norton	0.5
Reliance	0.25
Seyval Blanc	0.5
Vignoles	0.5

Winery

Tasting room hours: open daily, NOON–8 PM.
Seating: approximately 50.

Rainbow at Plainview Vineyard. *Courtesy of Plainview Vineyard.*

Wine	Style	Grapes
Red		
Chambourcin	All styles	Chambourcin
Léon Millot	Dry	Léon Millot
Maréchal Foch	Dry	Maréchal Foch
Norton	Dry	Norton
Concord	Sweet	Concord
White		
Seyval Blanc	Dry	Seyval Blanc
Vignoles	Semisweet	Vignoles
Other		
Blush	Semisweet	Traminette, Reliance

Other

Grape juice for home winemakers and fruit wines are for sale in the winery.

Contact and Directions

10456 Second Road, Plainview, IL 62685. (618) 836-5514. Chip.becker@yahoo
.com. The winery is 22 miles east of Highway 55 at the 52-mile marker on Highway 16.

ROUNDHOUSE WINE COMPANY

Owner

Sheila Kapes

History

This is one of the newer wineries in Illinois, near Centralia. It boasts the Trestle
Pavilion, a venue for celebrations and events. The tasting room for this winery,
opened in 2011, is the home where the family lived and raised children.

SAMPLE OF GRAPES GROWN

Grape Name	Acreage
Chambourcin	0.5

Winery

Tasting room hours:
Monday–Thursday, NOON–6 PM;
Friday–Saturday, 11 AM–
MIDNIGHT; Sunday, 11 AM–6 PM.
Seating: Trestle Pavilion seats 200
with room for 100 on the patio. The
tasting room seats 40 indoors and
40 on the patio.

Roundhouse Wine Company's pavilion at night. *Courtesy of Roundhouse Wine Company.*

Other

There are items for sale and live music events. They also sell wines from other wineries on the Heartland Rivers Trail.

Contact and Directions

1938 Dogwood Lane, Centralia, IL 62801. (618) 532-1600.

SAMPLE OF WINES PRODUCED

Wine	Style	Grapes
Red		
Chambourcin	Dry	Chambourcin
Roundhouse Red	Dry	Chambourcin, Norton
Little Caboose	Sweet	Chambourcin, Norton
Other		
Golden Spike	Semisweet	Apple

SPRINGERS CREEK WINERY

Owner

Colette André

History

Springers Creek began operations in 2007 and remains a storefront boutique winery. Their tasting room was once a grocery store. The winery building is right on Route 66, and appears in the Route 66 Hall of Fame. The winery is also very enthusiastic about being on the Mountain Bike Trail. The winery has two buildings and two gardens.

Sample of Grapes Grown
This winery does not grow its own grapes.

Winery
Tasting room hours: Thursday–Saturday, NOON–10 PM; Sunday, NOON–7 PM. Seating: 150.

SAMPLE OF WINES PRODUCED

Wine	Style	Grapes
Red		
Lincoln Head	Dry	Pinot Noir
Grapeful Red	Sweet	Zinfandel, pomegranate
Mother Road Red	Sweet	Merlot, raspberry
White		
Golden Girl	Dry	Pinot Grigio
Harvest Moon	Semisweet	Blend
Orchard Hill	Sweet	Riesling
Other		
Route 66	Blush	Blend

Springers Creek Winery's garden. *Author's collection.*

Other

Locally made jewelry is for sale at the winery. The winery is also near Madison County Transit Bike Trail.

Contact and Directions

817 Hillsboro Avenue, Edwardsville, IL 62025.
(618) 307-5110.
cmandre55@hotmail.com.
The winery is on Highway 157—the legendary Route 66.

Springers Creek Winery. *Author's collection.*

⊂ℨ

TUSCAN HILLS WINERY

Owners

Wes Pitcher, Wanda Pitcher, Brandon Waddell, and Amanda Waddell.

History

The winery stands on eight picturesque acres that formerly belonged to the Kollmeyer farmstead from 1860. Tuscan Hills opened their doors in 2011, and this dream of a local farm family has become a success. All their wines are blends and offer various ranges of sweetness levels.

SAMPLE OF GRAPES GROWN

Grape Name	Acreage
Marquette	0.8

Winery

Tasting room hours:
Sunday, 1 PM–6 PM;
Monday–Thursday, NOON–7 PM;
Friday–Saturday, 11 AM–11 PM.

Other

The owners currently host a series of social events for the Effingham area including Murder Mystery dinners, wedding parties, and comedy shows. Festivals take place throughout the year.

SAMPLE OF WINES PRODUCED AT THIS AWARD-WINNING WINERY

Wine	Style	Grapes
Red		
Chambourcin	Dry	Chambourcin, Corot Noir
Starry Night	Dry	Norton, Maréchal Foch
Sweet and Wild	Medium sweet	Corot Noir, Chambourcin, Concord, Maréchal Foch
Sweet Sicilian	Sweet	Chambourcin, Concord, Maréchal Foch
White		
Chardonel	Dry	Chardonel
Andiamo	Off dry	Seyval Blanc, Cayuga White
Other		
Pretty in Pink	Sweet blush	Catawba, Concord

Contact and Directions

2200 Historic Hills Drive, Effingham, IL 62401. (217) 347-9463. winemaker @EffinghamWinery.com. The winery is 1.7 miles off I-57. Go to the I-70 intersection, exit 162.

Tuscan Hills Winery. *Courtesy of Tytia Habing Photography.*

VAHLING VINEYARDS AND WINERY

Owner
Dennis Vahling and Brenda Vahling.

History
This winery employs many hands to produce wines from their own grapes. They are featured at several events throughout the area and Illinois and host many local events on the premises.

Sample of Grapes Grown
Grapes include Chambourcin, Concord, and Steuben.

Winery
Tasting Hours: May–December, Tuesday–Saturday, 10 AM–5 PM; Sunday, NOON–5 PM. January–April, Tuesday–Saturday, 10 AM–5 PM; closed Sunday.

Other
Cheese and crackers are available.

Contact and Directions
2683 County Highway 6, Stewardson, IL 62463. (217) 682-5409. sales@vahling vineyards.com. Between Mattoon and Effingham, near Stewardson, Illinois. Exit 160 from I-57 and I-70. Turn north on Route 32 and travel 7½ miles to Road 400 N; turn west and travel 1¼ miles to the winery.

Vahling Vineyards and Winery wine featured at Oak Park's Uncork Illinois. *Courtesy of Elliot Weisenberg.*

Wine	Style	Grapes
Red		
Chambourcin	Dry	Chambourcin
Friar's Favorite	Off dry	Blend
Fireside Red	Semidry	Chambourcin, Rougeon
Steuben	Semisweet	Steuben
White		
White Satin	Off dry	Blend
Prairie White	Semidry	Blend
Prairie Mist	Semisweet	Blend
Prairie Dawn	Sweet	Niagara

VILLA MARIE WINERY

Owner
Judy Wiemann

History
Villa Marie began as a family venture and still holds firm to the traditions handed down. John Drost and Mary Grizio's daughter founded Villa Marie to honor the memory of her parents. John was a semiprofessional baseball player and served thirteen years as mayor of Maryville. The Villa Marie 2,000-square-foot complex is a testament to the legacy of the two "locals" who instilled in their daughter love of the land and of their community. Judy also owns Piasa Winery and Pub.

Sample of Grapes Grown
Grapes include Chambourcin, Chardonel, Norton, and Traminette.

Winery
Tasting room hours: Tuesday, 11 AM–6 PM; Wednesday, 11 AM–9 PM; Thursday, 11 AM–6 PM; Friday–Saturday, 11 AM–11 PM, Sunday, NOON–7 PM.

SAMPLE OF WINES PRODUCED

Wine	Grapes
Red	
Pleasant Ridge	Corot Noir
Chambourcin	Chambourcin

Villa Marie Winery wines. *Courtesy of Villa Marie Winery.*

Other

The winery hosts numerous events such as weddings, banquets, and the Holiday Sweater event.

Contact and Directions

6633 E. Main Street, Maryville, IL 62062. (618) 345-3100. wine@villamarie1 .com. Eighteen miles from St. Louis, Missouri. Take I-55 to I-70 and exit 15B.

WILLOW RIDGE VINEYARDS AND WINERY

Owners

Louie Donnel and Tina Donnel

History

The Donnels are the original owners, and they opened their doors in 2007. Previously the property was farmland that had been in the family for over 150 years. The winery boasts a handcrafted bar, Tuscan-style atmosphere, stained glass windows, and a stone fireplace.

Other

Some retail items are for sale in the winery.

Contact and Directions

Route 2, Box 343A, Shelbyville, IL 62565. (217) 738-2323. willowridgewinery @pwr-net.coop. The winery is 7 miles northwest of Shelbyville.

SAMPLE OF GRAPES GROWN

Grape Name	Acreage
Chambourcin	0.5
Frontenac Gris	0.5
Maréchal Foch	0.5
Niagara	0.5
Vidal	0.5
Vignoles	0.7

Winery

Tasting room hours:
Wednesday–Thursday and
Saturday, 10:30 AM–5:30 PM;
Friday, 10:30 AM–6:30 PM;
Sunday NOON–5:30 PM.
Seating: tasting room, 50;
banquet room, 170.

SAMPLE OF WINES PRODUCED

Wine	Style	Grapes
Red		
Capella	Dry	Maréchal Foch
Chambourcin	Dry	Chambourcin
Maréchal Foch	Semisweet	Maréchal Foch
Harvest Red	Sweet	Concord
Hodson Hills	Sweet	Maréchal Foch
White		
Equinox	Dry	Geisenheim
Vignoles	Semisweet	Vignoles
Solstice	Semisweet	Geisenheim
Traminette	Semisweet	Traminette
Harvest White	Sweet	Niagara
Other		
Sunset	Semisweet blush	Traminette, Norton, Niagara

Willow Ridge Vineyards and Winery's building. *Courtesy of Willow Ridge Vineyard and Winery.*

THE WINERY AT SHALE LAKE

Owners
David Wesa and Susan Wesa

History
Shale Lake was founded in 2006 on the site of the Mt. Olive and Staunton Coal Company Mine #2 in Williamson, Illinois, by David Wesa and Susan Wesa. The mine operated from 1904 through 1957. The property was restored to pasture condition in 1990. Shale Lake consists of 211 surface acres with stables, pastures, vineyard, winery, lake, hiking trails, and cabins. The vineyard was planted in 2007, and the tasting room and winery were opened in September 2010.

SAMPLE OF GRAPES GROWN

Grape Name	Acreage
Cayuga White	1.2
Chambourcin	3
Maréchal Foch	3
Norton	1.8
Traminette	2
Vignoles	3

Winery
Tasting room hours:
Friday, 4 PM–10 PM;
Saturday, 1 PM–10 PM;
Sunday, 1 PM–6 PM.
Seating: inside, 35; patio, 43; outside, 100.

SAMPLE OF WINES PRODUCED

Wine	Style	Grapes
Red		
Decade	Dry	Chambourcin blend
Quarter Turn	Dry	Norton style
Beginner's Luck	Semidry	Chambourcin
Apostle	Sweet	Norton
Fifth Dimension	Sweet	Maréchal Foch
White		
Eleventh Hour	Dry	Cayuga White
Snake Eyes	Dry	Traminette
Cloud Nine	Semisweet	Chambourcin
Seventh Heaven	Semisweet	Vignoles
Sixth Sense	Sweet	Cayuga White
Other		
Triple Vine	Semisweet blush	Blended blush

The Winery at Shale Lake logo. *Courtesy of The Winery at Shale Lake.*

Other
Food, beer, and gifts are available in the winery.

Contact and Directions
1499 Washington Avenue, Williamson, IL 62088. (618) 637-2470. shale@madison telco.com. From I-55, take exit 37 west into Livingston. Turn right on Livingston Avenue heading north and travel 1.8 miles. Shale Lake will be on the right as the road turns west.

SOUTHERN *Region*

Southern Region Wineries

1. Alto Vineyards
2. Bella Terra Winery
3. Blue Sky Vineyard
4. The Bluff's Vineyard and Winery
5. Cache River Basin Vineyard and Winery
6. GenKota Winery
7. Hedman Orchard and Vineyards, Inc.
8. Hickory Ridge Vineyard and Winery
9. Hidden Lake Winery and Banquet Center
10. Hogg Hollow Winery, LLC
11. Honker Hill Winery
12. Jo-Al Winery and Country Store
13. Kite Hill Vineyards
14. Lau-Nae Winery
15. Lincoln Heritage Winery
16. Lyn-Nita Vineyards, LLC
17. Monte Alegre Vineyard and Cellars
18. Orlandini Vineyard
19. Owl Creek Vineyard
20. Pheasant Hollow Winery
21. Pomona Winery
22. Rustle Hill Winery
23. Schorr Lake Vineyards
24. Shawnee Winery Cooperative
25. StarView Vineyards
26. Von Jakob Vineyard
27. Walker's Bluff Vineyard
28. Windy Hill Vineyard and Winery

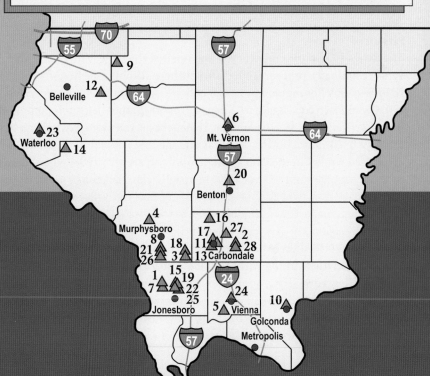

Alto Vineyards. *Courtesy of Megan Presnall/IGGVA.*

ALTO VINEYARDS

Owners

The Renzaglia family

History

The Renzaglia family constructed and opened the winery in 1988. This family venture has had a profound effect on southern Illinois. The first plantings were thanks to Guy Renzaglia, a professor at Southern Illinois University Carbondale (SIUC), and two colleagues, who began growing grapes in Illinois commercially (in 1982). Their idea was to plant native American and French American hybrids to adapt to Illinois' climate. The first vintage sold in 1986 to the Kohler family at Lynfred winery in the Chicago metropolitan area. By 1988 (when there were only five wineries in the state), the Renzaglia clan had constructed a six-hundred-square-foot winery. One problem was that the Village of Alto Pass was "dry," which made it very difficult to make wine—a vestige of Prohibition. With some persuasion, the law was lifted, and single liquor licenses were legalized.

Although the current owner, general manager, and winemaker, Paul Renzaglia, began life working with troubled youth after getting his administration of justice degree at SIUC, upon his return to the area his father convinced him to join the family wine business. He continues to innovate and think of ways to improve Illinois wine. In 2012 Alto Vineyards harvested its first vintage of *Vitis vinifera* varietals such as Albariño and Lemberger grapes.

SAMPLE OF GRAPES GROWN

Grape Name	Acreage
Albariño	0.5
Cabernet Franc	0.5
Carbernet Sauvignon	0.5
Chambourcin	2.25
Chardonel	1
Lemberger	0.5
Vidal Blanc	2
Vignoles	0.5

Winery

Tasting room hours:
Monday–Thursday, 10 AM–5 PM;
Friday–Saturday, 10 AM–7 PM;
Sunday, NOON–7 PM.
Seasonal hours apply.
Indoor and outdoor seating
accommodations.

SAMPLE OF WINES PRODUCED AT THIS AWARD-WINNING WINERY

Wine	Style	Grapes
Red		
Chambourcin	Dry	Chambourcin
Norton	Dry	Norton
Rosso classic	Dry	Chancellor, Chambourcin
Dawg House Red	Semidry	Chambourcin, Corot Noir
Heartland Red	Sweet	Concord
White		
Chardonel	Dry	Chardonel
Villard Blanc	Dry	Villard Blanc
Traminette	Semidry	Traminette
Vidal Blanc	Semidry	Vidal Blanc
Wiener Dog	Semidry	Vignoles, Villard Blanc, Vidal Blanc, Chardonel
Vignoles	Semisweet	Vignoles
Other		
Porto di Guido	Sweet	Chambourcin

Other

Items sold in the winery include T-shirts, sweatshirts, wine accessories, gift items, and a variety of cheese and sausage. By the time of the printing, there will be a new six-thousand-square-foot tasting and event facility indoor facilities with a patio overlooking the vineyard.

Guy Renzaglia at Alto Vineyards. *Courtesy of Alto Vineyards.*

Contact and Directions
Two locations: 8515 Route 127, Alto Pass, IL 62905. (618) 893-4898. inquiry @altovineyards.net. On the west side of Highway 127 in Alto Pass, 12 miles south of Murphysboro and 8 miles north of Jonesboro. Also: 4210 N. Duncan Road, Champaign, IL 61822. (217) 356-4784.

*G*uy began a trend. Seeing his success, other vintners in this area—Owl Creek, Pomona—decided to open their doors. Thanks to these pioneers and a few others, Shawnee Hills Wine Trail and the Shawnee Hills AVA were created in 1995. Viticulture in Illinois was now on the map, and the University of Illinois system began offering classes. Also, the vintners banded together and created the first incarnation of what is now the Illinois Grape Growers and Vintners Association.

BELLA TERRA WINERY

Owner
Edward Russell

History
The winery began in 1996, but the building was constructed in 2005. Currently total acreage is 166. The property was formerly used to raise cattle. The owners planted the first vineyard in 2000, and majestic trees still grace the landscape. The facility has picnic tables and a bocce ball court. All wines are made from their own grapes.

SAMPLE OF GRAPES GROWN

Grape Name	Acreage
Chambourcin	2.5
Concord	1
Seyval Blanc	1
Traminette	2
Vidal Blanc	2.5
Vignoles	2.5

Winery
Tasting room hours: open daily, 11 AM–6 PM. Seating: inside, 110; outside, several hundred.

Contact and Directions
755 Parker City Road, Creal Springs, IL 62922. (618) 658-8882. wine@bellawinery.com. The winery is 7 miles east of IL 24; use exit 7.

Other
Items for sale in the winery include beer, wine, sangria, and mixed drinks. Hookups for recreational vehicles, a bocce ball court, horseshoes pits, catch-and-release fishing, kennels, a hitching rack for horses, a pavilion, and a fire pit all enhance the experience. The winery is two miles from Tunnel Hill Bike Trail.

Bella Terra Winery. *Courtesy of Bella Terra Winery.*

SAMPLE OF WINES PRODUCED

Wine	Style	Grapes
Red		
Rubino	Dry	Chambourcin
Tunnel Hill Red	Semidry	Chambourcin
Tuscan Rose	Sweet	Concord
White		
Diamante	Dry	Vignoles
Tunnel Hill White	Semidry	Vignoles
Other		
Perta Rosa	Semisweet	Chambourcin
Bene Sera	Semisweet	Vidal Blanc, Seyval Blanc
Bacca Rosato	Sweet	Chambourcin

BLUE SKY VINEYARD

Owners

Barrett Rochman and Jim Ewers

History

Barrett has owned the ground where the winery stands for over thirty years. The owners had the idea of "planting a few grapes" in the late 1990s, and the winery was born. They planted the first two acres in fall 2000, adding a few acres each year through 2005. They broke ground for the winery in November 2003 and opened their doors on the 4th of July, 2005.

SAMPLE OF GRAPES GROWN

Grape Name	Acreage
Cabernet Franc	1.06
Chambourcin	3.57
Chardonnay	0.49
Corot Noir	1.10
Niagara	0.94
Noiret	0.98
Norton	1.06
NY 760844.24	1.03
Traminette	1.25
Vignoles	1.75

Winery

Tasting room hours:
Monday–Thursday, 11 AM–5:30 PM; Friday–Saturday, 11 AM–7 PM; Sunday, NOON–7 PM.
Seating: inside, 75; plus lawn and patio area with both shade and sun.

Blue Sky Vineyard. *Courtesy of Blue Sky Vineyard.*

SAMPLE OF WINES PRODUCED

Wine	Style	Grapes
Red		
Cabernet Franc	Dry	Cabernet Franc
Chambourcin	Dry	Chambourcin
Norton	Dry	Norton
Rocky Comfort Red	Sweet	Blend
White		
Chardonnay	Dry	Chardonnay
Rocky Comfort White	Sweet	Blend
Other		
Norton	Port style	Norton
Rosé	Off dry	Noiret
Papa's Rosa	Off dry blush	Chambourcin

Other

Items for sale in the winery include deli sandwiches, soups, pizza, cheeses, crackers, T-shirts, hats, other gift shop items, sodas, and beer. They also have two suites above the winery and a lovely waterfall, gazebo, and event facility perfect for weddings, business meetings, or gathering for any occasion.

Contact and Directions

3150 S. Rocky Comfort Road, Makanda, IL 62958. (618) 995-9463. bluesky @bluesky.com. From Carbondale, take Illinois Ave (US 51) south and turn left onto East Pleasant Hill Road. Turn right onto Giant City Lodge Road. Turn left onto Grassy Road. Turn right onto Rocky Comfort Road.

The Bluff's Vineyard and Winery. *Author's collection.*

THE BLUFF'S VINEYARD AND WINERY

Owners
Cheryl Ellis and Steve Ellis

History
One of the newer wineries in southern Illinois, this facility overlooks dramatic bluffs. They host numerous events as well as have their own tasting room and outdoor seating area.

SAMPLE OF GRAPES GROWN

Grape Name	Acreage
Cayuga White	0.5
Traminette	1

Winery
Tasting room hours:
Monday–Thursday, NOON–6 PM;
Friday–Sunday, NOON–8 PM

Other
The winery has a terrace overlooking the surrounding countryside and hosts events.

Contact and Directions
140 Buttermilk Hill Road, Ava, IL 62907. (618) 763-4447. info@thebluffswinery .com. Approximately 1 mile north, toward Chester, on Route 3 from the Route 149 intersection. The gate is ⅛ mile off Route 3—go straight up the hill.

Wine	Style	Grapes
Red		
Buttermilk Hill Red	Dry	Cabernet Franc, Cabernet Sauvignon, Chambourcin
Niagara	Semisweet	Niagara
Concord	Sweet	Concord
White		
Buttermilk Hill White	Dry	Chardonnay, Chardonel, Seyval Blanc, Vignoles
Riesling	Dry	Riesling

CACHE RIVER BASIN VINEYARD AND WINERY

Owner

Jack Dunker

History

Cache River Basin has been in operation since 1999. This facility is the southernmost winery on the trail, with ninety-seven acres of beautiful land that includes cypress trees, tupelo trees, and wetlands.

Cache River Basin Vineyard and Winery. *Courtesy of Cache River Basin Vineyard and Winery.*

Sample of Grapes Grown

The winery has seven varietals of grapes.

Winery

Tasting room hours: Friday, 4:30 PM–9 PM; Saturday, NOON–9 PM; Sunday, 11 AM–5 PM.

SAMPLE OF WINES PRODUCED AT THIS AWARD-WINNING WINERY

Wine	Style	Grapes
Red		
Hawktail Red	Dry	Maréchal Foch, DeChaunac, Chancellor
White		
Seyval	Dry	Seyval Blanc
Vignoles	Dry	Vignoles
Cache River Swamp Water	Semisweet	Seyval Blanc, Vignoles
Starbright	Semisweet	Seyval Blanc, Chardonel

Other

The winery includes Wineaux's Restaurant but considers itself a quiet haven, with few events to distract from the quiet surroundings.

Contact and Directions

315 Forman Lane, Belknap, IL 62908. (618) 658-2274. dunker@accessus.net. Take exit 14 for US 45 toward Vienna. Turn right onto US 45 S. Turn right onto Belknap Road. Turn left onto Forman Lane.

GENKOTA WINERY

Owners

Dr. and Mrs. Bradley Drake

History

This Amish-built winery overlooks two acres of vineyard. It opened its doors in 1997. The name stems from the couple's two daughters: Gennifer and Dakota. The winery perches on a sloping hill with beautiful trees surrounding the winery.

Other

The winery has a gift shop and hosts live music events.

GenKota Winery. *Courtesy of Karl Kageff.*

SAMPLE OF GRAPES GROWN

Grape Name	Acreage
Chambourcin	1
Villard Blanc	0.5

Winery

Tasting room hours:
June–September,
Monday–Thursday, 10 AM–6 PM;
Friday–Saturday, 10 AM–7 PM.

SAMPLE OF WINES PRODUCED AT THIS AWARD-WINNING WINERY

Wine	Style	Grapes
Red		
Norton	Dry	Norton
White		
Chardonel	Semidry	Chardonel
Vignoles	Semidry	Vignoles
Other		
Catawba	Blush	Catawba

Contact and Directions

301 N. Forty-Fourth Street, Mt. Vernon, IL 62864. (618) 246-9463. genkota @mvn.net Seventy-five miles from St. Louis, intersection of I-57 and I-64 in Mt. Vernon, Illinois.

Hedman's barn at Hedman Orchard and Vineyards, Inc. *Author's collection.*

HEDMAN ORCHARD AND VINEYARDS, INC.

Owner
Gerd Hedman

History
The winery started in 2005, but the locally famous peach orchard was the center of activity. The Hedmans still grow peaches, among the best in the state, two acres of which they also turn into wine. They also have wine grapes, ten acres to make mostly dry European wine. The pride of the winery is the three-story barn. It is in an area known for high-quality fruit. The winery is known for its Swedish charm.

SAMPLE OF GRAPES GROWN

Grape Name	Acreage
Cabernet Sauvignon	0.5
Chambourcin	2
Chardonel	2
Chardonnay	0.5
Corot Noir	1
Norton	1
Sauvignon Blanc	0.5
Seedless Concord	0.2
Traminette	2
Vidal Blanc	0.5

Winery
Tasting room hours:
January–April,
Friday–Saturday, 10 AM–9 PM;
Sunday, NOON–5 PM.
May–December,
Wednesday–Thursday, 10 AM–5 PM;
Friday–Saturday, 10 AM–9 PM;
Sunday, NOON–5 PM.

Wine	Style	Grapes
Red		
Chambourcin	Dry	Chambourcin
White		
Chardonel	Dry	Chardonel
Villard Blanc	Dry	Villard Blanc
Traminette	Semisweet	Traminette
Vidal Blanc	Semisweet	Vidal Blanc
Other		
Rosé	Semisweet	Chambourcin

Other

Scandinavian souvenirs, gourmet cheese, and other items are available in the winery. The Hedmans serve Swedish cuisine in their restaurant. This winery is also known as the Peachbarn Café, serving authentic Swedish cuisine.

Contact and Directions

560 Chestnut Street, Alto Pass, IL 62905. (618) 893-4923. peachbarn@aol.com. On Route 127, exit at Bald Knob Road, then turn left.

HICKORY RIDGE VINEYARD AND WINERY

Owners

Ron Presswood and Sylvia Presswood

History

The vines for this vineyard were started in 2000, with the first harvest and wine coming in 2003. As they expanded, the tasting room opened in 2007. The Presswoods have owned the land since 1979. Still today, the Presswoods use only their own grapes when making the wines they sell. The winery is perched on a forty-acre property. The interior decorations show that the Presswood family has extensively traveled and brought back souvenirs of their voyages.

Contact and Directions

1598 Hickory Ridge Road, Pomona; P.O. Box 507, Cobden, IL 62920. (618) 893-1700. The winery is 1 mile south of Pomona Winery. Take IL 127 north from Jonesboro and south from Murphysboro to Pomona.

Hickory Ridge Vineyard and Winery. *Author's collection.*

SAMPLE OF GRAPES GROWN

Grape Name	Acreage
Cabernet Franc	0.5
Cabernet Sauvignon	0.25
Cayuga White	0.25
Chambourcin	2
Norton	2
Petite Verdot	0.25
Traminette	1

Winery

Tasting room hours: spring–fall, Wednesday–Sunday, NOON–6 PM; Saturday, 10 AM–6 PM. Winter, Friday–Sunday, only by appointment. Seating: inside, 20; outside, 50.

SAMPLE OF WINES PRODUCED AT THIS AWARD-WINNING WINERY

Wine	Style	Grapes
Red		
Cabernet Franc	Dry	Cabernet Franc
Chambourcin	Dry	Chambourcin
Norton	Dry	Norton
Other Side	Dry	Norton, Chambourcin
Widow's Kiss	Dry	Chambourcin, Cabernet Franc
Herta's Blush	Sweet	Chambourcin
White		
Traminette	Dry	Traminette
2	Semisweet	Traminette, Cayuga White
Other		
Hankie's Trail	Dry blush	Chambourcin

HIDDEN LAKE WINERY AND BANQUET CENTER

Owners
Dale and Angie Holbrook

History
The secluded winery was established in 2008 in a beautiful, quiet forest setting.

Sample of Grapes Grown
The winery grows its own grapes.

Winery
Tasting room hours: Sunday–Thursday, 11 AM–5 PM; Friday and Saturday, 11 AM–MIDNIGHT.

SAMPLE OF WINES PRODUCED AT THIS AWARD-WINNING WINERY

Wine	Style	Grapes
Red		
Forest Hill Reserve	Dry	Chambourcin
Rocky Ford Red	Dry	Chambourcin
Double Decker Red	Semisweet	Catawba, Fredonia
White		
Pink Catawba	Sweet	Catawba

Hidden Lake Winery and Banquet Center. *Author's collection.*

Other

The winery can host banquets and has live music events. Its restaurant grill is also available for food and other beverages.

Contact and Directions

10580 Wellen Road, Aviston, IL 62216. (618) 228-9111. hiddenlakewinery @yahoo.com. Between I-64 and Route 5.

HOGG HOLLOW WINERY, LLC

Owner

Steve Hogg

History

This is a small family-owned winery with four generations involved in the operations. In the spring of 2004, they planted Norton grapes, and in winter 2005, Chambourcin. That year they opened the winery. Steve Hogg, the vintner, started producing wine the "old-fashioned way" over thirty years ago from the wisdom of friend Kay Bennett. Steve took classes in vineyard maintenance and wine production at Shawnee College in 2002, which brought the creation of Hogg Hollow Winery in September 2005, with the help of family and friends. The winery started in a small building, with a larger tasting room added in 2007.

Hogg Hollow Winery, LLC. *Courtesy of Hogg Hollow Winery, LLC.*

Sample of Grapes Grown

Grapes include Chambourcin, Chardonel, Norton, Seyval Blanc, Vignoles, and Villard Blanc.

Winery

Tasting room hours:
January–February,
Friday and Saturday, NOON–DARK.
March–December,
Thursday–Saturday, NOON–6 PM;
Sunday, noon–5 PM.

Hogg Hollow Winery, LLC, crest. *Courtesy of Hogg Hollow Winery, LLC.*

SAMPLE OF WINES PRODUCED

Wine	Style	Grapes
Red		
Norton	Dry	Norton
Vintner's Choice	Off dry	Norton, Chambourcin
Sweet Red Boar	Sweet	Chambourcin
White		
Chardonel	Dry	Chardonel
Seyval	Dry	Seyval Blanc
Vidal	Dry	Vidal Blanc
Other		
Shelby Rose	Semisweet	Chambourcin, Norton

Other

The gift shop sells natural grape juice, canned heirloom vegetables, and souvenir items. Barnyard animals entertain guests. You can sip wine while gazing over the pond, the vineyard, and the sunset. The tasting room is available for weddings, class reunions, birthday parties, and other gatherings.

Contact and Directions

48 E. Glendale Road, Golconda, IL 62938. (618) 695-WINE, cell (618) 521-0307. Off Highway 145 near Glendale, between Dixon Springs and Eddyville.

Grapevines at Honker Hill Winery. *Courtesy of Karl Kageff.*

HONKER HILL WINERY

Owners
The Lucas brothers

History
This family-owned winery and vineyard has been run by the Lucas brothers ever since they purchased the ninety acres in 1980. In 2004 they established the vineyard, and in 2008, the winery, so they could hand-process the grapes. The winery officially opened to the public in 2009. In 2012 this was the newest winery on the Shawnee Hills Wine Trail. In Williamson County, surrounded by the Shawnee National Forest, the facility boasts a fireplace, pond, and gazebo for year-round enjoyment.

SAMPLE OF GRAPES GROWN

Grape Name	Acreage
Chambourcin	3

Winery
Tasting room hours:
Friday–Sunday, NOON–6 PM.

Other
The winery hosts music events.

Contact and Directions
4861 Spillway Road, Carbondale, IL 62901. (618) 549-5517. Take I-57 to Highway 13, then go south on IL 148, west at County Road 25, and north on County Road 23.

SAMPLE OF WINES PRODUCED

Wine	Style	Grapes
Red		
Wally's Red	Semidry	Blend
White		
Villard Blanc	Dry	Villard Blanc
Other		
Honker Hill Blush	Semisweet	Blanc

JO-AL WINERY AND COUNTRY STORE

Owners
Jody Justus and Al Justus

History
This is one of only two wineries in Illinois to produce only fruit wines. This winery opened its doors in 2010. This tasting room and country store are named for the two owners: Jody and her husband, Al.

Jo Justus with Jo-Al Winery and Country Store wines. *Courtesy of Karl Kageff.*

Sample of Grapes Grown

This winery does not grow its own grapes.

Winery

Tasting room hours: Tuesday–Sunday, 10 AM–6 PM. Seating: 30.

SAMPLE OF WINES PRODUCED

Wine	Style	Fruit
Jonathan Apple	Semidry	Apples
Peach	Semisweet	Peaches
Blackberry	Sweet	Blackberries
Strawberry	Sweet	Strawberries

Other

The country store sells consigned jewelry, salsa, Beeswax Hand Cream, wine glasses, candles, cheesecakes, Illinois Dips and Soups, and gifts baskets, among other items. Many items are locally made. The gift shop offers samples of many items. Their sangria has very pronounced tropical flavors.

Contact and Directions

10213 State Route 177, Mascoutah, IL 62258. joalwinery@yahoo.com. (618) 566-WINE (9463). Take exit 23 off I-64 south, then drive 5 minutes for 5 miles.

KITE HILL VINEYARDS

Owners

Barbara Bush and Jim Bush

History

Natives of the southern suburbs of Chicago, Jim and Barbara grew tired of the so-called rat race; Jim was a cable splicing technician, and Barbara was an executive event coordinator. The property formerly belonged to Marty and Deloris McNitt, from 1980 to 1997, when it was apple orchards, then to Don and Nell Spire, who owned the property from 1997 to 2006. The Bush couple bought the land as a winery and bed-and-breakfast in 2006. Legend has it that the former owner's wife was not apprised of the purchase of the winery and when she confronted her husband to ask why he had bought a vineyard, he said he wanted to fly a kite. The name stuck: Kite Hill.

Being new to grape growing, Barbara and Jim attended conferences, produced a first harvest, and went through some trial-and-error experimentation. The third year, they were asking the right questions, contributing to the discussion, and well on their way to their current success.

Kite Hill Vineyards. *Courtesy of Megan Presnall/IGGVA.*

SAMPLE OF GRAPES GROWN

Grape Name	Acreage
Cabernet Franc	0.5
Chambourcin	1
Chancellor	0.5
Chardonel	1
Traminette	0.5
Vignoles	0.5

Winery

Tasting room hours:
March–November,
Thursday, NOON–5 PM;
Friday NOON–6 PM;
Saturday, 10 AM–5 PM;
Sunday, 10 AM–6 PM; Monday,
NOON–5 PM; also by appointment.
December–February,
Friday–Sunday, NOON–5 PM;
also by appointment.

Wine	Style	Grapes
Red		
Cabernet Franc	Dry	Cabernet Franc
Chambourcin	Dry	Chambourcin
Chancellor	Dry	Chancellor
Red Kite	Sweet	Blend
White		
Chardonel	Dry	Chardonel
Traminette	Dry	Traminette
White Kite	Semisweet	Traminette
Other		
White Chambourcin	Blush	Chambourcin

Other

Kite Hill Wine Slushies are very popular in summer: Grapevine Ice (a frozen blend of Grape Vine Ice Stir package mix and Kite Hill red or blush wine) and Peach Bellini (a frozen blend of Peach Bellini package mix and Kite Hill Vineyards white wine). The tasting room has an outdoor patio overlooking a lake famous for its turtle population. Kite Hill Vineyards has a two-room bed-and-breakfast, a gift shop, and an event center.

Contact and Directions

83 Kite Hill Road, Carbondale, IL 62903. (618) 684-5072. wine@kitehill vineyards.com. Take Route 13 west to Old Route 13, turn left and go west to Route 127, and turn left to go south 4.5 miles to Grammer Road.

LAU-NAE WINERY

Owner
Matt Mollett

History
The winery was established in 1999, and Matt Mollett has been producing wines since 2007. The winery's name derives from the owners' mothers' maiden names: Laurent and Naeger. It was the seventeenth winery to open in the state of Illinois. Lau-Nae produces its own wines plus serves wines from around the world.

Sample of Grapes Grown
Grapes include Catawba, Cayuga White, Chardonel, Concord, Maréchal Foch, and Niagara.

Lincoln Heritage Winery's tasting room. *Courtesy of Lincoln Heritage Winery.*

SAMPLE OF WINES PRODUCED AT THIS AWARD-WINNING WINERY

Wine	Style	Grapes
Red		
Vintner's Reserve	Dry	Corot Noir
Rail Splitter	Semisweet	Corot Noir
Two Rivers	Sweet	Corot Noir
White		
Riesling Reserve	Dry	Riesling
Water Tower	Semisweet	Riesling
Egyptian Gold	Semisweet	Riesling
Other		
Misty Rose	Semisweet	Corot Noir, Riesling
Ruby Red	Semisweet	Riesling, Blackberry juice

Contact and Directions

772 Kaolin Road, Cobden, IL 62920. (618) 833-3783. LincolnHeritageWinery @hotmail.com.

Lyn-Nita Vineyards' winery building. *Courtesy of Karl Kageff.*

LYN-NITA VINEYARDS, LLC

Owner
Anita Eckhardt

History
Anita Eckhardt yearned for a space to grow vegetables, but she wound up with something more. The winery is one of the newest in southern Illinois, opening its doors in November 2010. With the first set of grapes planted summer 2011, the Eckhardts and Fritts are beginning to bottle using estate grapes, grown on three acres north of town, to produce their wines. In the meantime, they're learning the ins and outs of the production process.

SAMPLE OF GRAPES GROWN

Grape Name	Acreage
Catawba	0.25
Chambourcin	1
Chardonel	0.5
Concord	0.125
Kimrod	0.33
Reliance	0.33
Villard Blanc	0.25

Winery
Tasting room hours:
Thursday–Sunday, NOON–6 PM;
Saturday, 11 AM–7 PM.

SAMPLE OF WINES PRODUCED

Wine	Style	Grapes
Red		
Chambourcin	Dry	Chambourcin
Norton Select	Dry	Norton
Elk Barn	Semisweet	Chambourcin, Norton
White		
Chardonel	Dry	Chardonel
Villard Blanc	Semidry	Villard Blanc
Elk Barn White	Semisweet	Traminette
Prairie Flowers	Sweet	Cayuga White
Other		
Prairie Winds	Sweet	Chambourcin Rose

Other
Items for sale in the winery include conserves, spreads, salsa and honey, art, ceramics, woods, metals, glass, hand-painted wine glasses and crystal stemware, handcrafted wine rack, and custom gift baskets.

Contact and Directions
514 Coal Road (US Highway 51), Elkville, IL 62932. (618) 568-1719. lynnitawinery @gmail.com. On Highway 51, 12 miles north of Carbondale, 5.2 miles south of Du Quoin, just south of Elkville.

MONTE ALEGRE VINEYARD AND CELLARS

Owner
C. David Ponce-Campos

History
Monte Alegre Vineyard and Cellars has been in business since 1987 and can thus be considered one of the first vineyards in the southern Illinois area. C. David Ponce-Campos has brought many of the souvenirs from his native Peru to adorn the shop adjacent to the vineyards. Nestled just behind a commercial area of Carbondale, Monte Alegre has brought its wine-making expertise to other wineries in the area. The winery is in a former horse farm and polo pony training center. The vineyard was originally planted in 1995, and wines are made from grapes grown on the farm. All wines are processed on location in the Ponce Cellars.

Monte Alegre Vineyard and Cellars. *Courtesy of Monte Alegre Vineyard and Cellars.*

SAMPLE OF GRAPES GROWN

Grape Name	Acreage
Carbernet Franc and other vinifera	0.5
Chambourcin	1
Chardonel	0.33
Frontenac	1
Norton	0.5
Seyval Blanc	0.33
Traminette	0.33
Vidal Blanc	0.33

Winery

Tasting room hours:
Wednesday–Saturday,
1 PM–6:30 PM;
Sunday, 2 PM–6:30 PM.
Seating: tasting room, 10.

Other

Handcrafts and souvenirs are sold in the gift shop, many of them from the owner's native Peru.

Contact and Directions

473 Ponce Trail, Carbondale, IL 62901. (618) 549-3952. david@poncecellars .com. On Route 13, go east from Carbondale 1½ miles to Reed Station Road, then go north ¼ mile to the winery sign on the left-hand side. Follow signs to the vineyard and winery entrance.

SAMPLE OF WINES PRODUCED

Wine	Style	Grapes
Red		
Chambourcin	Dry	Chambourcin
Fond de cave	Dry	Chambourcin, Norton
Norton	Dry	Norton
White		
Chardonel	Dry	Chardonel
Vidal Blanc	Semidry	Vidal Blanc
Other		
Liquid Poetry	Sweet Port style	Frontenac
Dawg Daze Rosé	Semisweet	Frontenac, Labrusca

ORLANDINI VINEYARD

Owner
Noella Orlandini

History
This vineyard was started in 1988, one of the early pioneers of Illinois wine. Orlandini is on one of southern Illinois' highest ridges in a beautiful location. The winery was licensed to sell in 2001, and still today two generations of the family work on the property. The winery is surrounded by lovely old-growth trees and has a pond nearby, all part of the rural charm of this location. The founder of Orlandini Vineyard, Gary Orlandini, passed away December 2, 2013.

SAMPLE OF GRAPES GROWN

Grape Name	Acreage
Chambourcin	3
Vignoles	1

Winery
Tasting room hours: April–November, Friday, NOON–6 PM; Saturday, 10 AM–6 PM; Sunday, NOON–6 PM. December–March, Friday, NOON–5 PM; Saturday, 10 AM–5 PM, Sunday, NOON–5 PM.

Other
Although Orlandini Vineyard does not serve food, visitors enjoy bringing picnic baskets. "Nonna's sangria" is quite popular as well.

Contact and Directions
410 Thorn Lane, Makanda, IL 62958. (618) 995-2307. orlandinivines@yahoo.com. From I-57, it is 10 minutes west from exit 36 and 12 minutes from exit 48.

Orlandini Vineyard's winery building. *Courtesy of Karl Kageff.*

SAMPLE OF WINES PRODUCED AT THIS AWARD-WINNING WINERY

Wine	Style	Grapes
Red		
Chambourcin	Dry	Chambourcin
Rosso Gustoso	Semisweet	Chambourcin
Saluki Red	Sweet	Chambourcin
White		
Saluki White	Semisweet	Riesling
Vignoles	Dry	Vignoles
Vignoles	Sweet	Vignoles

OWL CREEK VINEYARD

Owner
The Genung family; Brad Genung, winemaker

History
Brad has been involved in both the investment and production side of the wine business for almost two decades. Brad has an MBA in finance and an undergraduate education that includes chemistry and physics coursework. He is Owl Creek's winemaker and a leading advocate of super-premium wine production in the region.

Owl Creek first sank roots in 1980, when founder Ted Wichmann planted the first commercial wine grape vineyard in the region. Those same vineyards are the foundation of their wines.

The next chapter in Owl Creek's story begins with the Genung family taking over production of the wines in 2005. Ted remained focused on his first love—growing great wine grapes. Ted and his wife, Sarah, still tend the vineyards outside the winery door to this day. Brad Genung shared Ted's devotion to producing high quality wines and the integrity to focus on local varietals. When Genung took over Owl Creek, the winery was producing three thousand gallons per year. In a few short years, production is closer to twelve thousand gallons.

Sample of Grapes Grown

Grapes include Cayuga, Chambourcin, Chardonel, Concord, Niagara, Seyval Blanc, and Vignoles.

Owl Creek Vineyard. *Courtesy of Owl Creek Vineyard.*

$\mathcal{T}$ed was instrumental in launching the first winery in the region a few years later—Alto Vineyards in 1988. As a shareholder in Alto and the first commercial winemaker in the region, Ted, along with the Renzaglia family, led the renaissance of the local wine industry. As a part of that rebirth, Ted built Owl Creek's winery in 1995 and cofounded the Shawnee Hills Wine Trail that same year. In 2002 he was instrumental in establishing the Shawnee Hills AVA.

Winery

Tasting room hours: March–December, Monday–Thursday, NOON–5 PM; Friday, NOON–6 PM; Saturday, 10 AM–6 PM; Sunday, NOON–6 PM. January–February, Thursday, NOON–5 PM; Friday, NOON–5 PM; Saturday, 10 AM–5 PM; Sunday, NOON–5 PM.

SAMPLE OF WINES PRODUCED AT THIS AWARD-WINNING WINERY

Wine	Style	Grapes
Red		
Owl's Leap	Dry	Chambourcin, Norton
Bald Knob	Semisweet	Chambourcin
Ruby Red	Sweet	Concord
White		
ChardonOwl	Dry	Chardonel
Water Valley White	Dry	Niagara (old growth)
Seyval Blanc	Semidry	Seyval Blanc

Other

March through December the café is open on weekends. There is a Saturday Music Series, 2–6 PM every Saturday, April–June and September–October. The winery serves food only on weekends, but they welcome picnic baskets.

Contact and Directions

2655 Water Valley Road, Cobden, IL 62920. (618) 893-2557. Near Cobden between I-57 and Route 51.

PHEASANT HOLLOW WINERY

Owners

Bruce Morgenstern and Bill Needham; Denny Franklin, winemaker

History

Nestled over five acres of scenic woodlands on Rend Lake in a rustic setting, and with a porch and a stone fireplace, Pheasant Hollow provides a lovely atmosphere to enjoy wine.

Sample of Grapes Grown

This winery does not grow its own grapes.

Winery

Tasting room hours: Monday–Saturday, 10 AM–6 PM; Sunday, NOON–6 PM.

Other

The winery hosts a Cajun festival and Murder Mystery nights.

Contact and Directions

14931 State Highway 37, Whittington, IL 62897. (618) 629-2302. info@pheasant hollowwinery.com. Take exit 77 off I-57, go east on Route 37, turn left, then immediately turn left onto the winery's lane.

Pheasant Hollow Winery's tasting room. *Courtesy of Karl Kageff.*

Wine	Style	Grapes
Red		
Ringneck Red	Off dry	Chambourcin
White		
Vignoles	Semisweet	Vignoles
Other		
Amanda's Blush	Semisweet	Vidal Blanc, Chambourcin
Pink Catawba	Semisweet	Catawba

POMONA WINERY

Owners
George Majka and Jane Payne

History
The current owners purchased the winery in 1991 and released their first wine in 1993. Pomona was the sixth winery to open in Illinois and one of the founding wineries of the Shawnee Hills Wine Trail. They specialize in non-grape wines and use locally grown fruit in all of them. Surrounded on three sides by the Shawnee National Forest, they use the nickname "peace and quiet winery." They serve no food, have no entertainment, but do give every customer an in-depth wine tasting complete with food-pairing suggestions and recipe ideas.

George Majka of Pomona Winery. *Courtesy of Midwest Wine Press.*

Sample of Grapes Grown
All wines are made from the fruit of their own orchard.

Winery
Tasting room hours: December–March, Friday–Saturday, 10 AM–5 PM; Sunday, NOON–5 PM. April–November, Monday–Saturday, 10 AM–5 PM; Sunday, NOON–5 PM. Seating: outdoor covered seating, 30; indoor tasting room space, 40.

Pomona Winery's building. *Courtesy of Karl Kageff.*

Other

The winery participates in many festivals.

Contact and Directions

2865 Hickory Ridge Road, Pomona, IL 62975. (618) 893-2623. pomonawinery @wildblue.net. Take Highway 127 to Pomona Road, then go west 0.8 mile to Sadler Road, then turn right. Go left on Jerusalem Hill Road, then 2.4 miles. Turn right on Hickory Ridge Road, then continue 2.5 miles.

SAMPLE OF WINES PRODUCED AT THIS AWARD-WINNING WINERY

Wine	Style	Fruit
Jonathan	Semidry	Apples
Golden	Semisweet	Apples
Once in a Blue Moon	Sweet	Blueberries
Peach	Dessert	Peaches

RUSTLE HILL WINERY

Owners

John Patrick and Debra Russell

History

The winery, established in 2008, is one of the newer additions to the southern Illinois wine arena. Rustle Hill has sixty acres of land for growing grapes and for the expansive winery and concert facility. The facility also includes an amphitheater, three bandstands, five cabins, a full-service restaurant (including catering), an art gallery, and a gift shop.

SAMPLE OF GRAPES GROWN

Grape Name	Acreage
Chambourcin	1.5
Villard	1
Zinfandel	0.5

Winery

Tasting room hours:
Sunday–Thursday, NOON–7 PM;
Friday and Saturday, NOON–9 PM.

SAMPLE OF WINES PRODUCED AT THIS AWARD-WINNING WINERY

Wine	Style	Grapes
Red		
Chambourcin	Dry	Chambourcin
Norton	Dry	Norton
White		
Seyval Blanc	Dry	Seyval Blanc
Vidal Blanc	Dry	Vidal Blanc
Traminette	Semisweet	Traminette
Sweet Seyval	Sweet	Seyval Blanc
Other		
White Chambourcin	Semisweet	Chambourcin
Sweet Chambourcin	Sweet	Chambourcin
Dessert Chambourcin	Dessert port	Chambourcin

Other

Rustle Hill has more than 250 concerts a year, as well as numerous other events in its amphitheater. It has five cabins available, with a capacity of more than thirty people overnighting on the premises. The restaurant is open 363 days a year and caters to full-service lunch and dinner every day. A rotating art gallery schedule brings a new local artist into the gallery every two months for a perpetual show.

Rustle Hill Winery. *Courtesy of Karl Kageff.*

Contact and Directions

8595 New Highway 51, Cobden, IL 62920. (618) 893-2700.
aaron@RustleHillWinery.com. Take Highway 51 10 miles south of Carbondale
to Cobden.

SCHORR LAKE VINEYARDS

Owner
Paul Nobbe

History
This winery officially began in 1994 with a section of seven acres of vineyard.
They also still grow blackberries. The winery was bonded in 1997 and officially
opened in 1998. Many family and friends have helped with various aspects of
the enterprise. The property has a lovely lake, picnic tables, and many birds.
All wines are estate grown and produced.

Sample of Grapes Grown
The winery grows sixteen varieties of grapes on seven acres.

Winery
Tasting room hours: Friday–Sunday, NOON–6 PM.

Schorr Lake Vineyards tasting room. *Courtesy of Karl Kageff.*

Other

The winery can host parties and events.

Contact and Directions

1032 S. Library Street, Waterloo, IL 62298. (618) 939-3174. Fifteen miles south of St. Louis, along Highway 3, 10 miles east of the Mississippi River.

SAMPLE OF WINES PRODUCED

Wine	Style	Grapes
Red		
Cynthiana	Dry	Cynthiana
Chambourcin	Semisweet	Chambourcin
Catawba	Sweet	Catawba
White		
Seyval	Dry	Seyval Blanc
Vidal Blanc	Semisweet	Vidal Blanc
Niagara	Sweet	Niagara

SHAWNEE WINERY COOPERATIVE

Owner
Cooperative

History
In 2004 this cooperative was formed to create a market for Illinois wines. They received major support from the USDA and the state of Illinois for their endeavor.

Sample of Grapes Grown
This winery does not grow its own grapes.

Winery
Tasting room hours: January–March, Monday–Saturday, 10 AM–5 PM; Sunday, NOON–5 PM. April–December, Monday–Saturday, 10 AM–6 PM; Sunday, NOON–6 PM.

SAMPLE OF WINES PRODUCED AT THIS AWARD-WINNING WINERY

Wine	Style	Grapes
Red		
Shawnee Red	Dry	Chambourcin, Frontenac
White		
Shawnee White	Dry	Seyval Blanc, Chardonel
Dream Catcher	Sweet	Concord, Niagara

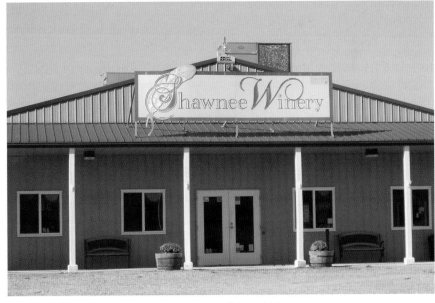

Shawnee Winery Cooperative. *Courtesy of Amy Alsip.*

Contact and Directions

200 Commercial Street, Vienna, IL 62995. (618) 658-8400. greatwine@shawnee winery.com. Take Highway 24, exit 16. Follow IL 146 to Industrial Drive and take a right to Commercial Street.

STARVIEW VINEYARDS

Owner

Ron Dalius, Susan Dalius, Brett Morrison, and Regina Morrison

History

The winery opened in 2005. Brett is not sure about previous owners but is pretty sure the land used to be used for cattle grazing. StarView built a new tasting room in 2006. They have 7.5 acres of grapes and bottle eight to ten thousand gallons of wine a year. The winery has a wood fireplace, a wraparound deck, and a koi fish pond for guests to enjoy.

SAMPLE OF GRAPES GROWN

Grape Name	Acreage
Chambourcin	1
Chardonel	1
Niagara	0.25
Norton	1
Seyval Blanc	1.5
Vignoles	1.5

Winery

Tasting room hours:
Summer, Monday–Thursday, 11 AM–6 PM; Friday, 11 AM–7 PM; Saturday, 10 AM–8 PM; Sunday, NOON–7 PM.
Winter (November–March), Monday–Friday, 11 AM–5 PM; Saturday, 11 AM–7 PM; Sunday, NOON–5 PM. Seating: 200.

SAMPLE OF WINES PRODUCED AT THIS AWARD-WINNING WINERY

Wine	Style	Grapes
Red		
Norton	Dry	Norton
Super Nova	Dry	Chambourcin
Red Giant	Dry	Noiret
Red Star	Semisweet	Chambourcin
White		
Chardonel	Dry	Chardonel
Seyval	Off dry	Seyval Blanc
Vignoles	Off dry	Vignoles
Niagara	Semisweet	Niagara
Vidal Blanc	Semisweet	Vidal Blanc

Sign for StarView Vineyards. *Courtesy of Karl Kageff.*

Other

Items for sale in the winery include wine accessories and food. The winery also hosts many events.

Contact and Directions

5100 Wing Hill Road, Cobden, IL 62920. (618) 893-9463. Take Highway 51 to Wing Hill Road.

VON JAKOB VINEYARD

Owners

Dr. Paul and Rhoda Jacobs

History

There are now two wineries in the same area from these owners, the first established in 1996 (the year they planted their grapes). They are also justly famous for their orchards. The couple opened the tasting room in 1997. They expanded to their second location in Alto Pass, Illinois, in 2003. With the beautiful orchard they purchased, filled with peach trees and other fruit, they were able to offer a line of fruit wines as well. Von Jakob was the fourth winery on the Shawnee Hills Trail and boasts the first Cabernet Sauvignon grown and bottled in Illinois.

Von Jakob Vineyard. *Author's collection.*

SAMPLE OF GRAPES GROWN

Grape Name	Acreage
Carbernet Sauvignon	3
Chambourcin	3
Chardonnay	1.5
Traminette	4
Vidal Blanc	4

Winery

Tasting room hours: Alto Pass location (spring, summer, and fall), Monday–Thursday, 10 AM–5 PM; Friday, 10 AM–6 PM; Saturday–Sunday, 10 AM–7 PM. Winter, Monday–Thursday, 10 AM–5 PM; Friday–Sunday, 10 AM–6 PM. Seating: 700.
Pomona location, Saturday, 10 AM–5 PM; Sunday, NOON–5 PM. Seating: indoor (including two ballrooms), over 500; outdoor (including two decks), over 60.

Other

Von Jakob Brewery is now open. The property also has five suites to rent in the bed-and-breakfast. There is also a large gift shop.

Contact and Directions

Alto Pass location: 230 Highway 127 N., Alto Pass, IL 62905. (618) 893-4600. Von Jakob Vineyard, 1309 Sadler Road, Pomona, IL 62975. (618) 893-4500. info@vonjakobvineyard.com. Fifteen miles south on 127 from Murphysboro.

Wine	Style	Grapes
Red		
Chateau Red	Dry	Maréchal Foch, Chancellor, Chambourcin
Country Red	Sweet	Maréchal Foch, Chancellor, Chambourcin
Ridge Red	Sweet	Concord
White		
Cave Creek	Dry	Vidal Blanc
Hillside White	Semidry	Vidal Blanc
Traminette	Semidry	Traminette
Canyon Gold	Sweet	Vidal Blanc
Other		
Late Harvest	Dessert	Vidal Blanc

WALKER'S BLUFF VINEYARD

Owners

Cynde Bunch and David Bunch

History

In October 2009 Walker's Bluff opened its doors with the Legends Restaurant. The property was purchased eighty years before by the owners' grandparents. The property currently hosts dinners and events and has a general store and a tasting room. For a time they received wine-making assistance from other wineries in the area but as of this writing have moved to their own bottling, processing, and aging facilities. Since 2013, they have worked toward adding a lodge/spa and "glam" camping site.

Sample of Grapes Grown

Grapes include Barbera, Pinot Gris, Sagrantino, Sangiovese, Syrah, and Tempranillo.

Winery

Tasting room hours vary.

Sample of Wines Produced

The winery produces several wines but serves wines from around the country and the world in its restaurant.

Walker's Bluff Vineyard tasting room exterior. *Courtesy of Karl Kageff.*

Other

The winery has a reputation for fine dining, as well as attracting major musical groups.

Contact and Directions

326 Vermont Road, Carterville, IL 62918. (618) 956-9900. From I-57, take exit 54B to DeYoung Street/IL 13; turn right at Reed Station Road, to Vaughn Road, then County Line Road.

WINDY HILL VINEYARD AND WINERY

Owner

Wayne Wagner

History

This winery opened in November 2007, one of the newest in this part of Illinois. The family-owned winery is run by Scott Wagner and his father, Wayne Wagner. They have four acres of grapes on a forty-acre farm, from French hybrid to native American grapes. They belong to the Southern Illinois Wine Trail. Their logo, representing a Native American march, was created by a cousin who lives in St. John, Indiana. The winery enjoys a country atmosphere, with birds plentiful. There's also fishing and other activities on the premises.

SAMPLE OF GRAPES GROWN

Grape Name	Acreage
Catawba	1.5
Cayuga White	0.5
Chambourcin	1
Concord	4 rows, 100 feet long
Niagara	2 rows, 100 feet long
Vignoles	1

Winery

Tasting room hours:
Wednesday–Saturday, NOON–5 PM;
Sunday, 11 AM–5 PM.
Seating: inside, 16; front porch, 8;
side patio, 20.

Other

Items for sale in the winery include mulling spices, glasses, paintings, grape vases, and flower pots. The winery hosts a bed-and-breakfast and much more.

Contact and Directions

2955 Creal Springs Road, Creal Springs, IL 62922. (618) 996-3581. Between Creal Springs and Tunnel Hill at Creal Springs Road, 18 miles south of Marion, 5 miles south of Creal Springs, and 3 miles north of Tunnel Hill.

Windy Hill's vineyard. *Courtesy of Megan Presnall/IGGVA.*

SAMPLE OF WINES PRODUCED

Wine	Style	Grapes
Red		
Chambourcin	Dry	Chambourcin
Catawba	Sweet	Catawba
Red Feather	Sweet	Concord, Catawba
White		
Cayuga	Semisweet	Cayuga White
Vignoles	Semisweet	Vignoles
Other		
Chambourcin	Blush dry	Chambourcin
Enchantment	Sweet	Chambourcin, blackberry
Wind Dancer	Blush sweet	Catawba, strawberry

GLOSSARY
INDEX

Glossary

Grapes typically found in Illinois wines are featured in chapter 3 and will not be repeated here.

acidity. A characteristic taste of wine. All wines contain some level of acidity, although white wines tend to have higher acidity than reds.

alcohol. A by-product of fermentation.

alluvial. Soil created by the erosion of water. Most Illinois soil is at base alluvial, deposited when the glacier retreated.

aroma. The wine smells inherent to the grape and the fermentation methods. Tasters often comment on the aroma.

AVA (American Viticultural Area). Region identified for its grape growing and discernible by geographic features. At least 85 percent of the grapes grown in the region must be used to produce wine, but there is no restriction on type, yield, or method of wine making. In California, for example, Napa is an AVA. The first Illinois AVA was the Shawnee Hills AVA, in Southern Illinois near Carbondale. There is now a second AVA, the Upper Mississippi River Valley AVA, the largest in the United States. Besides Illinois, it includes regions of Minnesota, Wisconsin, and Iowa.

barrel. A wooden container to age and store wine. Many red wines in Illinois, although not all, are aged in barrels.

barrel aging. Aging wines in barrels, by which tannins and depth are increased. This benefits primarily red wines.

black rot. A fungal disease detrimental to grapes and other crops; it is common in Illinois.

blind tasting. Serving wines with labels covered so guests don't know their origin. This way, a wine's reputation has less influence on the taster.

body. The heaviness or lightness of wine in your mouth, its density.

Botrytis cinerea. A fungus that attacks grapes when the skin opens on the vine. It can be beneficial on certain types of grapes if a winemaker wishes to make sweet dessert wines. It is very detrimental, however, if a winemaker is aiming for a dry wine.

bouquet. More complex smells than those involved in "aroma."

carbonic maceration. A type of fermentation using whole bunches of grapes in a closed container. This keeps wine fresh and keeps the fruit flavors more pronounced.

chaptalization. Adding sugar to wine, thereby increasing alcohol and sweetness. This is allowed in Illinois but not in California, for example.

clone. In the case of grapes, a plant chosen because it has characteristics considered beneficial and that should therefore be passed on to future generations.

cold fermentation. Lowering grape juice to 55 degrees F to conserve as many primary and secondary fruit characteristics as possible in the wine.

corked. Said of wine that smells or tastes off, which signals the wine has gone bad, perhaps because the cork was defective. The increased use of screw caps or plastic corks was largely to address this defect of natural corks.

crown gall. A bacterial disease of grapes. Galls, or little bumps, form on the stems.

cultivar. A plant or group of plants selected for desired characteristics.

decant. Transfer of the wine from bottle to container (decanter, pitcher, glass) so the wine can breathe (aerate) or to eliminate sediment in older wines.

dry wine. Wine with low residual sugar content.

filtration. Removing all sediments. Some winemakers produce unfiltered wine because they perceive it as more natural, and some consumers do as well.

fining. Another clarifying technique for wine. While filtration is one of the last steps and is optional, fining is considered a necessary part of the wine-making process. This removes the more prominent cloudiness in wine.

finish. The last taste of the wine in your mouth. A long finish indicates a high quality wine.

flight (tasting). Tasting small portions of several different wines.

fortified wine. Sweet dessert wines with higher alcohol and higher sugar concentrations than table wines.

fruit forward. Having the fruit characteristics most prominent. Most Illinois wines tend to be produced as fruit forward wines, although most winemakers also believe in terroir (*see* terroir *below*). Not to be confused with "sweet" (*see* residual sugar).

grafting. One type of vine fuses to another creating a new plant.

hybrid. Genetically creating a grape from two other types, a *Vitis vinifera* with a *Vitis labrusca*, for example. This usually creates a more resistant grape. In Illinois, hybrid resistance to cold weather proves useful for allowing grapes to grow.

late harvest. When grapes stay on the vine for an extended period of time, usually to make the wines sweeter.

lees. The leftover skins, seeds, etc. at the bottom of the barrel, the end products of the fermentation process.

loess. A type of soil, extremely common in Illinois, created when glaciers retreated over the continent.

malolactic fermentation. A bacterial process that turns sharp malic acids in wine to lactic acids.

mildew (downy *and* powdery). Common fungal diseases. Their names indicate their appearance on the plants they attack.

must. The remnants of the fermenting process before arriving at sediment. This thick juice can sometimes be distilled to make higher alcohol content beverages.

nose. A wine's smell (*see also* aroma *and* bouquet).

oenologist. A scientific specialist of grape cultivation and wine making.

oxidized. Said of a wine that tastes bad because oxygen has affected it.

phenolics. A class of chemical compounds contained in grape skins. Tannins are a type of phenolics.

phylloxera. A louse, the worst pest to attack vineyards in the late nineteenth century. It still exists today, but we now know how to control it.

punt. The indentation at the bottom of the wine bottle.

racking. After fermentation, the transfer of wine from barrel to barrel to eliminate sediment.

Blue Sky Vineyard vista. *Courtesy of Megan Presnall/IGGVA.*

reserve. A term usually indicating a winemaker's most prized bottles. In many parts of the world, including the United States, the term does not have a precise, legal definition.

residual sugar. Sugar left in the wine after fermentation. This determines the wine's sweetness.

rootstock. The root bulb on which shoots from other vines are grafted.

rosé. Pink colored wine popular in many parts of the world. It can be made using several methods, such as mixing red and white juices or by allowing red grape skins to come in contact with white juice. Illinois rosé wines often use the term "blush" on the bottle.

sediment. Deposits in the wine bottle. These deposits contain elements that have precipitated out of the wine due to extended age, or because the wine had some residual elements left.

sommelier. Person in charge of the wine cellar, the spirits, and the cigar humidor in a restaurant.

sweet wines. *See* residual sugar; *by contrast, see* fruit forward.

tannins. Chemicals in wine, mostly red, that give it a bracing flavor.

tasting (vertical *and* horizontal). Event where several wines are tried one after the other. Horizontal tastings pair different wines of the same vintage; vertical tastings compare different vintages of the same wine.

terroir. An indefinable French word indicating how the earth creates the wine.

ullage. The air space at the top of a bottle or barrel.

varietal. Wine made primarily from one grape, usually named on the label.

vintage. The year the grapes used for a wine were harvested.

Vitis aestivalis. A genus and species of grape native to North America.

Vitis amurensis. A genus and species of grape native to Asia.

Vitis labrusca. A genus and species of grape native to northeastern North America (Concord, Niagara, etc.).

Vitis riparia (or *vulpina*). A genus and species of grape native to northeastern North America.

Vitis rotundifolia. A genus and species of grapes (Muscadine) native to the southern part of the United States.

Vitis rupestris. A genus and species of grape native to North America.

Vitis vinifera. Genus and species of grapes used for most quality wines, native to Europe.

Index

Italicized page numbers indicate photos.

❧

CLARA ORBAN is a professor of French and Italian and the chair of the Department of Modern Languages at DePaul University. She is also a certified sommelier and teaches a geography course based on wine at DePaul. Of her published books, one other is about wine: *Wine Lessons: Ten Questions to Guide Your Appreciation of Wine* (2012).